RECONNECTING
THE
LOVE ENERGY

Reconnecting the Love Energy

Don't By-Pass Your Heart!

Phyllis Krystal

SAMUEL WEISER, INC.

York Beach, Maine

First published in 1995 by
Samuel Weiser, Inc.
P. O. Box 612
York Beach, ME 03910-0612

04 03 02 01 00 99 98
10 09 08 07 06 05 04 03 02

Library of Congress Cataloging-in-Publication Data
Krystal, Phyllis.
        Reconnecting the love energy : don't by-pass your
    heart! / Phyllis Krystal.
            p. cm.
            ISBN 0-87728-849-6
        1. Sathya Sai Baba, 1926–.   2. Spiritual life—
    Hinduism.
        I. Title.
    BP1175.S385K78   1995
    294.5'44—dc20   95-36571
    CCP   CIP

Cover photo by Jane Fleishman.
Copyright © 1995 Jane Fleishman.

Typeset in 10 point Palatino

Printed in the United States of America

The paper used in this publication meets the minimum
requirements of the American National Standard for
Permanence of Paper for Printed Library Materials
Z39.48-1984.

*I dedicate this book to Sri Sathya Sai Baba,
whose heart overflows with love for all beings.*

Table of Contents

Part II
The Heart By-Pass in Public Institutions

Acknowledgments

First, I offer my sincere gratitude to Sri Sathya Sai Baba, for without his love and encouragement I would never have attempted to write. I also thank him for showing me the heart by-pass and for opening my heart and teaching me how to allow the universal love to flow through it to others.

I owe an enormous debt of gratitude to Peggy Lenney. With tireless enthusiasm she has patiently typed and re-typed this manuscript, as well as my previous ones.

I am also deeply grateful to my assistant, Susan Leh, for her invaluable help with this book and with all the other areas of my life so that I could devote time to writing.

I thank all those who have been involved in this publication so that I could present this book to Baba on his 70th birthday as he requested. But my special thanks go to Betty Lundsted for her interest and encouragement.

And last but not least, I thank my late husband Sidney for his support during the many years which allowed me to be productive in this way.

LOVE

Love is letting go
Not holding on.
Love is loving everyone
And not just some.

Love means demonstrating
What true love can do
By bringing joy to many
And not just one or two.

Introduction

Although at the time I was completely unaware of it, the basic theme of this book was given to me in a reverie or waking dream several years ago. I was working with a partner and consulting the inner wisdom or Hi C (Higher Consciousness) available within everyone. Usually, when working in this way, I would be given insight into a variety of problems I myself was facing, or those I had been asked to check for others to enable me to offer them methods to help themselves. However, on this particular occasion Sai Baba appeared on my inner scene as soon as I had closed my eyes in readiness to ask for guidance. His presence felt just as real to me as it is when I have been close to his physical form in India. And his voice was just as sweet to my inner ear as it is to all those who listen to his discourses at the ashram, on audio and videotapes, or in an interview.

He seemed to be beckoning me to follow him, but, of course, in thought only, and telling me that he was going to show me "the real heart by-pass." I assumed that he intended to teach me a new healing technique, but that proved not to be the case at all. As I mentally followed him, it was as if we were moving high up above the earth. Baba pointed to a huge human figure that appeared to be superimposed over the planet. It reminded me of the diagrams of the impersonal human body found in Yoga books. It was neither male nor female, and the chakras were clearly marked as wheels of light at the appropriate locations. At first, I thought Baba wanted to show me that the earth can be symbolized as a human form;

the macrocosm compared to our bodies that represent the microcosm. But I soon discovered that this was not his sole purpose, for he proceeded to deliver a discourse that flowed into my mind just as fast as I have heard him speak at the ashram. As I listened intently within, I felt great sympathy for his translators, who often have difficulty in keeping abreast of his fast flow of words, especially when he starts a new train of thought before they have had time to translate the previous sentences. It must require intense concentration on their part, just as I, too, experience when I receive his inner discourses.

He pointed to the chakras and indicated that they are all interconnected by pathways like beams of light, except for the paths leading to the heart. Those he showed me were either completely cut off, or partially blocked, leaving the heart chakra almost isolated from the others. It reminded me of the blocked arteries around the physical heart that need to be unblocked by a medical heart by-pass.

Very seriously and intently, he explained that this is the real heart by-pass at the world level, but the same condition is present on an individual or personal level in the majority of people in whom the heart, along with true caring, has been rejected. I was profoundly moved and close to tears by this graphic illustration, for I knew only too well how accurate it was. Yes, we have cut off contact with our hearts, or as Baba expressed it, we have "by-passed the heart."

He then outlined the steps, starting from way back in time, showing how this situation has gradually developed. He explained that in the beginning it was obvious to everyone that women gave birth to new human beings, the babies. The people concluded that the Great Creator, or God, should be worshipped in the form of a woman. I was reminded of the symbolic figurines uncovered during the various excavations of old cultures, of fertility goddesses fashioned with a protruding belly resembling a pregnant woman about to give birth to a baby. In those early days, Baba continued to explain, people were not yet as aware of the man's role in the creation of a new being, so the fertility goddess was worshipped as a symbol of God, the Great Creator. Later, when the warrior tribes began to infiltrate and conquer the more pastoral groups, they brought with them the concept that God must be sufficiently powerful to help them to overcome their enemies, so they worshiped a strong male figure.

The men of the various tribes waged war on other groups and hunted wild animals to feed their families. But while they were engaged in such apparently heartless pursuits, the women kept their hearts open and active in their role of bearing and nurturing their children. They were able to rekindle the caring qualities in their men when the latter returned to the family after fighting or hunting.

In time, as the men became even more powerful and warlike, the women were gradually and inexorably forced to occupy a more and more debased place in the tribe. They were reduced to being owned and controlled by men, and they were treated like possessions—sex objects or brood mares and on a par with the men's other possessions. Like animals, they were often used as beasts of burden. Under these unhappy conditions, women withdrew from their connection with their hearts and feelings because it became too painful to feel. So the universal heart by-pass increasingly and relentlessly continued to develop and operate worldwide over the succeeding centuries.

In recent years some of the more brave and aware women have begun to rebel against being classed as second or third-class citizens, or worse. They attempted to fight the situation by copying men. By primarily using logic, while ignoring their hearts and feelings, they furthered the development of the heart by-pass instead of remedying the imbalance in themselves and in their daily activities.

Baba proceeded to explain that the balance in the world needs to be restored by reactivating the heart, but it is the individual who will bring about the changes in the world. Women, who are the natural guardians of the heart energy, need first to open up their own hearts, and then they will be capable of reconnecting men to their hearts.

As Baba outlined all that needed to be done to correct this sad situation, it seemed like a formidable undertaking. But that is exactly why he is here and has assumed a human form, as avatars before him have done at such times when the world had reached a critical state of lovelessness, which is certainly the case now.

But even an avatar cannot work in a vacuum to bring about the changes that are so necessary. It is we, the people who have lived intermittently in the world as different personalities at different times over the expanse of many centuries, who have contributed to the present situation. We need to take responsibility for applying the remedies available as quickly as possible if catastrophes are to be avoided. Time is important if we are to save this civilization from annihilation. A worldwide catastrophe could occur due to our lack of awareness of the seriousness of the imbalance resulting from the universal absence of caring.

As this overall survey of the present situation was being so dramatically unfolded, I was deeply moved, as I instinctively knew how frighteningly correct it was.

At some level of my being I was undoubtedly aware that I was not being given this vision unless I, too, would be willing to participate in finding ways to solve some of the problems, and thereby remedy the widespread dilemma. But I must admit that at the time I had no thought of writing yet another book, let alone this one. I would have forcefully resisted such an idea as being far too enormous a task to undertake, especially at my advanced age and with my travel schedule involving seminars on the Cutting the Ties Method, and talks at Sai conferences and centers so rapidly increasing. It was not until now, several years later, that I received definite instructions from Baba to write this book.

But before that time, and a few years after I had received this vision, during a group interview Baba suddenly announced to the gathering, "Mrs. Krystal is writing another book." It was the furthest thing from my mind even at that time. But the book to which he was referring was *Taming Our Monkey Mind*, and he undoubtedly foresaw that it needed to be written before this one. I realize now that it was a forerunner to prepare the way for the heart energy to be reinstated. For, if our desires are too strong and our monkey minds are in control, we are still too self-involved to care about other people.

The Monkey Mind book has been published and presented to Baba. At that time I asked when I should return, which has been my habit each time I am with him. He smiled in a way that caused me to wonder what new surprise he was about to spring on me, and said, "Come next year for the 70th birthday celebration and bring a new book to present on that occasion." As he spoke, he rubbed his chest with his hand, so I asked if it was to be about the heart by-pass. With a big smile he said, "Yes, very happy." The 70th birthday was just a bare fifteen months away, certainly not much time to write and publish a book.

During my travels I have been made acutely aware that the world situation has steadily worsened. It has become desperately important for all of us to do whatever we can to help bring about a change, but we must do it first in ourselves. Then it will start to spiral out to others and eventually reach the world.

Baba had shown me the effect of the heart by-pass on both the world and the individual. I realized that the denigration of women involves the suppression of the feminine within each of us, in both men and women. The earth is the Universal Mother by whom all living creatures are nourished, and she, too, is suffering from neglect. In fact, rejection of the heart and our inability to care leads to defacement of the earth.

The balance of Yin and Yang, to use Chinese terms, has been revealed in the ancient teachings to be essential in all areas of life, not least in human beings. But at present the balance has been drastically disturbed. These two strong opposite poles, Yin being the negative, receptive, nurturing pole, and Yang, the positive, assertive, and active pole, are both essential for any type of creativity or action to take place. So, when the earth has been demeaned and maimed, the Sun, which symbolizes the Yang (or father principle) becomes too dominant on all levels, and dries up the waters of emotion.

"As above, so below," or as with the macrocosm so with the microcosm. When these two great forces of positive and negative energy lose the natural rhythm between them in the world, that same rhythm is lost in human beings, who, by their physical gender, are differentiated into primarily Yin or Yang. But each of us contains both Yin and Yang aspects—or heart and head. These two, on the microcosmic level, mimic the two great parents, Earth Mother and Solar Father on the macrocosmic level. As we demean the Yin (or feminine aspect) and elevate the Yang (or masculine), we add to the imbalance in ourselves as well as in the world.

Many people feel that, as individuals, they are too weak and ineffectual to help the world situation, for any help they might give would be like a mere drop in the ocean. But if many single drops are put together, the sum would be a mighty force. So the responsibility rests squarely on the shoulders of each of us, both men and women, to help correct the imbalance between these two great forces and thus bring about healing of the schism.

What are we all waiting for? Do we expect someone else to start the healing process so that we can then jump onto the band wagon when others have started it rolling? But, as with any other moving vehicle, by the time we decide to come aboard, it may be moving too fast for us to catch up with it; in which case, we may be left behind. Then, we may think that some exterior force caused that to happen and lament our bad luck or fate. But our fate would be due only to our own tardiness, our own timidity and cowardice, our own laziness, and, above all, our own selfishness in expecting others to do for us what we must do ourselves. Each one of us is responsible for our own part in the cure since we have all contributed to the problems.

In the work in which I have been involved for many years, I have lately become even more acutely aware of the important role of dedicated individuals. I have often heard a forlorn lament from someone who feels helpless to make a difference. This attitude is particularly prevalent among young people and is not limited to any single country. It is seen all over the world.

I have often been asked to give talks to groups of teenagers and young adults. I always happily accept, as I thoroughly enjoy meeting youth groups in various parts of the world. They are of the utmost importance as they will form the future population of each country, and will therefore be the ones who determine its destiny.

I have been impressed by the fact that in all the youth groups the same general questions and complaints were forthcoming. By far the most common statement has been that these young people are angry with their elders for causing the present state of the world, which they are now about to inherit. Since I always seek within to be given answers to such questions from my Real Self rather than from my brain, I sought within for an answer to this common complaint. I fully realized that I needed a solution that would not merely satisfy the particular group I was addressing, but preferably would give some direction on how to improve the situation about which they were so worried. The answer I received astonished me. The thought came rapidly to my mind that everyone who is alive at this present time, including all the children and young people, are equally responsible for the present state of the world. The reason I was given that this is, indeed, the case was that each one of us has, in every one of our many past lives, contributed, over many centuries, to negative thought forms that have accumulated so much energy that they are now controlling the world and everyone in it. So it is our responsibility, young people as well as older people, to do everything in our power to reverse the situation we have all caused with our past thoughts, emotions, words, and deeds. The responsibility is then placed exactly where it belongs, on every living person on the planet. It is clearly useless, as well as a sheer waste of time and energy, for any of us to blame others for a situation we have all helped cause.

So where can we begin? We do not need to rush out into the world and take on huge challenges. If we bring about changes in our own personal lives, it will act like the small amount of yeast needed to raise a large lump of dough, in preparation for making a loaf of bread. In this way, by our example, we can raise the consciousness of those with whom we come into daily contact. The way we live our lives can make others aware of what they, too, could do to help correct the world situation, instead of sitting back idly waiting for others to improve their lot for them.

Both individually and in groups we can all cooperate to bring about the necessary changes, so we need to scrutinize the many different areas of activity in which people are involved, as well as all our different relationships. This survey can show clearly where the "heart" has been omitted and the "head" has become too dominant in every area of life as we experience it now.

This book is a cry for help to all those who are truly dedicated to service, whether at the individual level or on a more widespread scale. It will take the commitment of as many willing people as possible to reverse the present trend toward destruction by re-instating the heart and with that, *re-connecting* the heart energy.

There is only one royal road
for the spiritual journey—Love.
—Baba

PART I

The Heart By-Pass in Personal Relationships

CHAPTER 1

HEART BY-PASS?

In order to clarify the meaning of the phrase, *heart by-pass*, as it is used in this book, the word heart and all that it signifies must first be examined and defined. According to Webster's dictionary, "the human heart is the seat of emotions, personality and attributes; the moral side of human nature in contradistinction to the intellect, as in 'he was all head and no heart.'"[1] When we think of the word heart, or hear it mentioned, various qualities come to mind, such as feeling, compassion, empathy, and love, whereas we connect thinking, logic, planning, organizing, and intellect with the brain.

The heart has become synonymous with love. For instance, "he or she has no heart" implies that the person being described is incapable of expressing love, while someone who is described as having a "heart of gold" signifies that this person is considered to be very loving. We even refer to someone we love as "sweetheart."

St. Valentine's Day is celebrated each year as a day on which to send and receive love. A custom of giving cards to mark this day is very popular, especially among young people. Most of the cards display a big red heart accompanied by greetings expressing love and sometimes love poems. Unfortunately, many of these cards are extremely sentimental and saccharine sweet and express an artificial emotion rather than true love.

While driving on today's highways, it is common to see bumper stickers that carry messages such as, "I love animals,"

---

[1] *Webster's New Twentieth Century Dictionary*, Second Edition.

or " I love skiing," or "I love gold," etc. The word "love" is symbolized by a big heart, since a heart and love are connected in many people's minds.

When we speak of the heart by-pass, or of by-passing the heart, it means that the feeling that is connected with the word "love" is cut off, or by-passed, and cannot be expressed.

We would be well-advised to check our behavior to see whether we express kindness, affection, caring, even politeness, to others. Our lives can become so full of mechanical activities that acts of kindness that come from the heart are crowded out.

Unexpected acts of kindness and consideration can have a much more far-reaching effect than we could imagine. They can start a chain reaction by affecting not only the people to whom they are given, but also everyone the recipients come into contact with throughout the day. Because of our acts of consideration toward others, their hearts may be opened, and they may be more inclined to give those they meet a smile, a kind word or a helpful hand.

CHAPTER 2

What is Love?

Since the heart by-pass indicates that the feeling called love is blocked in some way, it is also necessary to define the word "love" so we are clear about what is being by-passed. However, in order to try to determine its true meaning, it is easier to decide what it is not and thus examine some of the false concepts that have accumulated around this much maligned word.

Sai Baba says that most human love is selfish and contracting, whereas the love he has for everyone is unselfish and expansive. It would certainly appear that the motive for most human love is selfish. "What's in it for me? How does it make me feel? How will I be benefitted if I love this person? How can I change that one to fit my needs or desires? How will a relationship with this one affect my image? What do I need to do or say to persuade this one to love me?"

Many people, and men in particular, give gifts of material objects in lieu of love. They also equate the sexual act with love. But neither of these actions expresses love from the heart. The tendency to by-pass the heart often stems from traumatic experiences in childhood involving feeling that was linked to an unhappy event, such as the death of someone close–a parent, sibling, or friend. Many children will close off the heart when feeling proved to be connected to any type of pain.

When a parent has died or deserted the family, the remaining parent often attempts to make up for this loss by trying to be both mother and father to the children. But this often results in a too possessive or smothering relationship, which can become a problem when children receive the impression that love is being used to control instead of indicating genuine caring. When love has been confused in such ways, often only a trauma or some kind of control will evoke any emotion. At the same time, there is a need to shut off the negative feeling that is causing pain. The end result is one of emotional crippling and neither genuine sadness nor true happiness can be expressed. A low self-image is a frequent result and is demonstrated either by feelings of inferiority or the reverse–an overly superior attitude. Both reactions are concerned with the person's self-image and no amount of love will satisfy this profound need. Some people may become over-achievers, either pursuing intellectual success or some kind of physical prowess to prove that they are worthwhile or better than those who caused the lack of emotional support.

In other cases, people will act out the lack of self-worth in different ways. They may descend into deep depression, become aggressive, violent, self-destructive, or they may make desperate and unreasonable demands for love and affection. Others will fall into the habit of repeating the patterns they learned from parents and, in turn, are unable to express love. They may even mimic the same negative behavior they, themselves, received as children. Thus a chain reaction is established which will continue to operate indefinitely.

The above examples indicate selfishness and an overriding desire to own other people just as though people are possessions. It is based on "what I want, what is good for me or will satisfy my desires," with no consideration for the welfare of the so-called loved ones.

Some people profess love toward another person with a view to gaining a servant who will do their bidding and provide for all their needs. Both men and women may enter a relationship with this goal as their main motive.

A woman will look for a successful man who can provide her with security, social status, all the possessions she craves, the overseas travel she thinks will be so exciting, a good education for any children they may have, and, in addition, will shower her with love and affection. When any of these expected benefits are not forthcoming, she is bitterly disappointed and will often search for another man whom she hopes will satisfy her demands.

A man will seek an attractive woman with a pleasing personality who will enhance his own image, especially in connection with his occupation or profession. She should be a good hostess, a good mother to their children, be not merely good, but always available sexually, though not too demanding of his time or attention.

But where does the partner's needs enter into such a formula? And even more importantly, do these formulae have anything to do with love, which involves giving love and affection as distinct from needing or demanding it? Whenever we think we need something or someone to make us happy or satisfied, we immediately become a slave to that person, object, place, or idea.

Many relationships do not allow the partners the freedom to express themselves or to live according to who they are; these relationships require one partner to live at the other's bidding.

Then there is the kind of love that is actually more like an obsession, or addiction, and has little to do with real love. It has as its basis an exaggerated need for what the other person is expected to supply and is just as hard to break as any other addiction.

Con men pretend to love their chosen victims. They often seek out lonely older widows who are vulnerable to their protestations of love and who confuse it with real emotion. These unsuspecting women are devastated when their knights in shining armor abandon them, taking all their money, jewels, and other valuable assets, which were the reason these men professed love in the first place.

But it is not only men who indulge in such deceitful and hurtful behavior. Some women also are con artists and take advantage of an unsuspecting man by "taking him for all he is worth."

The pretence of love, with the hidden motive of lining one's own nest at the emotional as well as at the financial expense of another human being, has nothing to do with "love." It is selfishness expanded to a most cruel degree.

Baba has said that much of the love people express is really lust and not true love at all. Lust is an inordinate craving for something or someone. It is desire carried to an extreme. Love is letting go and lightly flowing, whereas lust is holding on and tightly grabbing.

I recall one time, when my husband and I were in India, Baba invited us to attend an evening of bhajan singing by his college boys, during which Baba delivered short discourses and stories. This particular evening he demonstrated the meaning of lust by acting out the way a student might catch sight of a juicy apple, grab it, and immediately start to devour it greedily, with undisguised relish, until it was all eaten. This action, Baba averred, was an example of lust. By a person's lust for it, the fruit becomes rajasic and inflames, arouses and intoxicates rather than remaining sathwic and conducive to equanimity, which is the true nature of an apple. Instead of remaining centered, we reach out too far, from too much desire for something, and lose our balance. This is also true of lust for another person. Physical lust is not love, but a determination to possess another and use control with the intent to bend that person to our will.

Sexual lust is one of the bodily appetites that arises from a physical urge to gratify the senses. It is essentially selfish since the needs or desires of the other person are ignored. It appears to be more easily aroused in men, and when uncontrolled can lead to extreme acts of violence, such as child abuse, rape, mayhem and even murder.

Sexual harassment and date rape are terms that have finally been brought to our attention by being widely publicized in the media. However, the media are also responsible for arousing lust in those who are exposed to the various forms of pornography and exploitation which present people as sex objects rather than as loving human beings.

Lust leads directly to the heart by-pass because it relates entirely to the physical body and its appetites and excludes love, affection, kindness, and consideration for the partner. The heart of the sexual aggressor is closed to the other's needs, and the victim's heart is also closed as protection against assault.

CHAPTER 3

LEARNING HOW TO LOVE

When contemplating on how and where to start to remedy the global heart by-pass, it became obvious that its influence is so pervasive that every aspect of human life needs to be inspected. That includes our lack of true feeling and its ultimate effect in every sphere of life.

Everything in life involves some kind of relationship, either with other people, objects, places, memories, experiences, and habits. We cannot live in a vacuum, even if we strive to reduce our connections or attachments to a bare minimum. Even in solitary confinement, or during an experiment with sensory deprivation, the participant relates to the jailor or facilitator, the cell, cage, or tank in which he or she is enclosed, as well as to every facet of daily experience and any reactions to them.

Viktor Frankel, in his book, *Man's Search for Meaning*[1], wrote that during his incarceration in a Nazi concentration camp, he came to realize that there was only one freedom left to him. It was the freedom to choose the attitude he should adopt toward everything that happened, and to those with whom he was involved, both guards and other prisoners.

He proved by his own personal experience that we are all free to choose how we react to external stimuli, both events and the various people with whom we interact.

In the reverie work, we have been instructed by the Hi C that everyone and everything in our lives can provide an op-

---

[1] Viktor Frankel, *Man's Search for Meaning* (New York: Touchstone, Simon & Schuster, 1984).

portunity to learn. If we are willing to stop blaming life, fate, God, or other people for our problems and ask what each person or experience can teach us, we can reap the benefit hidden within each day's challenges. We can choose to accept the teachings thus offered, or resist them and build up resentment. We can decide to be critical and judgmental, or loving and understanding. The choice is always our's, though many people are completely unaware of this fact. To understand it and put it into daily practice is to be free.

Many people repeatedly ask me how they can *re-connect* their hearts and learn to be more loving. They say that they do not know how, because they did not receive love from their parents. They were not shown either how to receive love or how to express it.

The young of all species learn by mimicking the behavior and actions of their parents. Human children have an additional ability not shared by other creatures, for humans can choose their reactions to outer stimuli. If children observe that their parents' behavior has a positive effect, they will copy it. But if the opposite appears to be the case, they will rebel against it, either overtly or inwardly. These early reactions can and often do determine adult behavior.

If children have been exposed to loving care by their parents, they will have learned from that positive early experience how to receive love, and can also be taught how to give it to others. In this way a habit or pattern is started in infancy that continues into adult life in the many different relationships that will be formed.

Unfortunately, many children lacked this early conditioning and grew to adulthood emotionally crippled and unable to give or receive love. Fortunately, no one needs to be permanently locked into this condition. A remedy was demonstrated to me in a very unexpected and dramatic way many years ago when my husband and I were flying from Bombay to London on a plane that was taken over by hijackers during the flight.

We learned much later that two Palestinians had boarded the plane in Beirut, where it landed briefly for refueling. They had bribed the food handlers, who were delivering the food, to hide guns and ammunition in one of the containers of food and place it beneath the seats reserved for them.

Of course none of the passengers or members of the crew were aware of this arrangement. Shortly after the flight attendants had served a meal and removed the trays, the two Palestinians entered the cockpit and took over the plane. One of them remained with the copilot, to supervise the flight from then on, while the pilot and all the first class passengers were told to move back into the tourist section where we were sitting. As they were passing us, my husband asked the pilot what was happening. He grimly answered that we would soon find out. As soon as they had all found seats, these two fierce-looking men appeared and asked if any of the passengers spoke both Arabic and English. One man raised his hand and in halting English translated what they were saying to him in Arabic. He reported that the plane was being hijacked and that no one was to move or talk and that if anyone needed to use the toilets, one of the flight attendants must be in attendance.

They then collected all the passports, handbags, and carry-on luggage. They leafed through the passports, and emptied the contents of the small bags, filled them with dynamite and placed them outside the toilets and at other strategic sites throughout the plane, with the intention of eventually setting fire to them.

As soon as all this started to unfold, I immediately called to Baba, urgently requesting him to help, and repeating his name and directing my pleas to the room in the building where he was staying, which we had just so recently left behind in Bombay.

As I continued my silent cries for help, I heard his voice in my head telling me to send love to the hijackers. As I looked at their exultant faces, which showed that they were obviously gloating over the terror they were causing their victims, I mentally answered, "I can't." Instantly, another thought entered my mind. "I can't send them love, but you can, for you are the only one who is always able to see the God-self in everyone, even in men like these two. You can love them, but I can't. So if you will send your love to me I will be willing to direct it to them."

From then on I concentrated on breathing in Baba's love and directing it to those two frightening looking men. I could actually feel it flowing into me. No, I personally could not love them, and in any case, my limited personal love would not have been as effective as the much more powerful love from Baba.

I was fascinated as I watched them become perceptibly more and more nervous. One of them was busily occupied in breaking all the bottles of liquor and perfume from the duty-free store and emptying the contents in the aisles to make it easier to set fire to the plane. As I continued to send him Baba's love, his hands started to shake so much that he cut his hand on the broken glass and had to stop to bandage it with a hand-kerchief.

Later that same year, when we returned to the ashram, Baba assured me that the plane had been filled with his love, which had saved all the passengers.

Notwithstanding my great relief at being spared, this experience was even more important in a quite different way. It demonstrated the tremendous power of love, and showed me that I need not feel helpless over my own personal lack of it as long as I would be willing to ask for this much more powerful variety to flow through me.

One of the ways to re-activate the heart is to breathe in this potent energy and direct it to all who need it. This exercise can be practiced alone, but is even more effective in a group, particularly if the symbol of the Maypole is used to connect each participant to the God-within or Hi C. This simple little exercise takes only a few minutes to practice, and can help anyone willing to use it to learn how to receive and then give love, even to those who appear to be unworthy of it, or so negative as to be closed to it. Instructions on its use can be found in the *Cutting the Ties that Bind Workbook*, published by Samuel Weiser.

CHAPTER 4

WE ARE ALL THREE PEOPLE

We have all been given opportunities to make choices and we can use this privilege either to work patiently to remove the layers that obscure the light within each of us, or we can continue to add more and more layers which will hide it even more completely from ourselves and from others.

Baba states that each one of us, in our present state of consciousness, is composed of three people. The one we know best, and therefore the one with which we identify, is our conscious awareness of the physical body, the ego, and the brain, with all of our memories stored within it as in a computer. Also part of this conscious self are our desires, which are connected with the five senses, our habits, behavior, and the programming imprinted upon us from early childhood by parents, family members, teachers, and friends. All of these are only temporary, for our use in the present life experience, and can be considered as teachers to help us learn the lessons we still need to be taught. But this small limited self is not the real one.

The second of the three selves to which Baba refers is the one other people observe. This, too, is not real or valid. Many people present a bold front to the world which is often at variance with the way they feel inside. In my own case, I was often told by others, and particularly by my mother, that I always gave the impression of being *as cool as a cucumber*. That may very well have been true of the outer façade I presented to the world, but it was in stark contrast to the way I felt inside, or how I saw myself behind that false mask. Inside, I was terrified and utterly insecure most of the time, never being sure what words, actions, or attitudes would prompt my mother to punish me severely.

I have observed that many people who appear to be bombastic, self-assured, or egotistic are attempting, by assuming this false front, to persuade others as well as themselves that they are adequate, worthwhile beings. Some people are very successful in fooling others with the perpetual act they choose to play in a vain effort to try to counterbalance their own sense of insecurity and low self-esteem. So it is often a case of, "me thinks he or she doth protest too much," as they struggle to free themselves from these false roles–the inferior one with which they identify, and the opposite one of apparent superiority–that they show to the world and wish were true. Neither role with which we identify is real or permanent. Both are merely composed of the overlay that has been built up around the inner spark of divinity which alone is real and lasting.

The third is the Real Self, which is love personified, but how can it be expressed through these thick layers of false self-concepts? This condition, shared by the vast majority of people, was once illustrated for me as a lamp symbolizing the Real Self covered by a lamp shade that was so thick that the light of the lamp was hidden, or at best, only barely visible beneath the heavy shade.

Another way of looking at our usual condition can be represented by an onion, composed as it is of many skins or layers that we need to remove so that the essence (or light) can be revealed. Only when this has been achieved will we become enlightened or Self-realized. To be Self-realized means that we are re-united with the light that we already are, and always have been, despite the fact that we have remained so long unconscious of our divinity.

The universal heart by-pass that was shown to me in the vision given by Baba in reality refers to the blindness that affects us and prevents us from accepting and expressing the Real Self. Instead, we identify with the masks that we mistakenly accept as real and permanent.

When we continue to live as if separate from the Hi C, we are cut off from the heart, which is the vehicle through which we receive love from the inner source. It is through the heart that this love can then flow out to all others, whether we happen to like their outer personalities or not. They, too, identify with their flawed personalities, but deep within is an identical spark of divinity that can be reached and re-ignited by the love from our own inner spark, just as many candles can be lit by one that is already alight.

In order to reverse the heart by-pass, we need to recognize and accept our own true Self so that we can become an instrument for It to make contact with the same reality in others. At that level of consciousness we are all one with It, and with everyone else. Only the outer sheath separates us from who we are, and, consequently, from all others.

By-passing the heart is equivalent to living separate from the Hi C. Our very essence is but a small part of the whole energy (or consciousness) that some people refer to as God. This inner essence—which is the only real part of everyone— is true love. That is Its nature and also Its action when It is allowed to flow freely from deep within each person and out to all living creatures, without exceptions, prejudices, or preferences.

Because most people are completely unaware of their true identity, or at best only partially in contact with It, the expression of love is blocked. Rejection or unawareness causes the personal heart by-pass, which in turn results in the universal or worldwide one.The only way we can correct this universal condition is to bring about the necessary reversal within ourselves. When such a correction is multiplied by more and more people, the urgently needed worldwide connection to the heart energy will be made possible.

Each one of us is responsible for the heartless conditions in the world. We have all contributed to this situation by our own lack of caring in this life, but also in many prior lives, and are now reaping the results of our past thoughts, feelings, words, and deeds.The result of such a lack of true feeling is frighteningly evident. We are more aware of our world because the media bombards us with information of such a sobering nature that we cannot avoid knowing about the universal breakdown in human affairs.

An antidote to such a dire situation is to reverse our former practice of seeking in the outer world for what we need and turning within, to the source, from which all our needs will be met. But "Seek ye first the kingdom of God, and his righteousness and all these things shall be added unto you,"[1] succinctly encapsulates this truth.

The reverie, or waking dream technique, which I have been guided to pursue for many years as part of my own search for meaning to life, offers one method we can use to bring about a reversal of the practice of expecting to be supplied with everything from the outer material world, instead of seeking it from the more reliable source within. This technique is presented in my *Cutting the Ties That Bind* books and workbook.

---

[1] St. Matthew 6:33, King James.

CHAPTER 5
___

"What Do You Want?"

___

Baba has a favorite question that he will suddenly shoot at someone, invariably at his or her first contact, whether in the darshan line or in an interview. "What do you want?" he will ask as he looks penetratingly at whoever he is addressing while intently awaiting an answer. Usually, the person being interrogated stutters and fumbles, not being certain what answer Baba expects. One person may announce with a self-satisfied expression, "I only want enlightenment," as if the speaker expects Baba to materialize something known as enlightenment and place it in an eagerly out-stretched hand, as Baba does with the articles he so easily manifests from time to time. But even that seemingly impressive answer is not the one Baba is hoping to hear. Another person will answer more honestly and directly by imploring Baba to provide something specific, such as a husband or wife, a cure for some illness, a baby, or maybe a job promotion. The desired boons are as varied as the people who ask for them.

But underlying all the answers, both those that are voiced in a vain attempt to impress Baba, as well as those that spring from an actual desire, what is the one essential that everyone needs?

Baba himself supplies the answer. He says, "I will give you what you want, hoping that at some time you will ask me for what I have come to give you, which is love."

Everyone hungers for love, though very few have a clear idea of what it is they are really seeking. To many it is merely an illusion, and like the elusive bluebird of happiness, it is always hovering enticingly just beyond their grasp.

From birth until death, love is often the missing ingredient we all crave and continue to seek, often in very strange and unsatisfying ways.

All young creatures need love as much, if not more, than they need food, for it is the special food that is essential in providing happiness and contentment.

The mother's love is the first experience of love to which a baby is exposed, and it thrives only if love is supplied in addition to food. Experiments with young animals have shown that even when they are fed a balanced diet, if they are deprived of the love of their mother, they will not develop fully, and will lack confidence and independence. Children who have been placed in orphanages or foster homes display similar symptoms, due to the same lack of love from their mothers.

Those who have never experienced satisfying love from their mothers when they were children continue to crave a mother's love, and strive to obtain it from other relatives, friends, partners, their own children, and other unsuspecting people. They look to others to fill their unrequited need, and frequently demand that it be satisfied. But to their repeated disappointment, the more they demand, the less others feel inclined to supply it. Even with more tangible gifts most people experience a feeling of hesitation about giving something to a person who is already expecting or even demanding it. Most people generally prefer to feel completely free, either to give or not to give, however they are inclined. When someone expects a gift, people often shy away from giving it, or give it grudgingly. People don't want to be with an adult who is still acting like a demanding child, so these undeveloped adults are often rebuffed and left with a pressing need to be mothered. The unsatisfied adult may turn to other sources to fill the void: liquor, food, sex, or candies to supply something sweet or comforting to allay their pain.

When people expect unconditional love, they place a heavy burden on those from whom they seek it, for no human being can give to someone else what he or she does not have to give. Human love is rarely unconditional. In most cases there are strings attached to it. Love is not a commodity to be bought and sold, bartered, or hoarded. It has to be allowed to flow freely without any kind of constraint, for only then can it be called love.

In our frantic quest for what we think we want, or what we think will make us happy, we really want to be special in some way to someone to prove that we are worthy of acceptance. But we must first believe in ourselves. Baba says, "Have faith in yourself. When you have no faith in the wave, how can you get faith in the ocean?"

No one is better than or worse than anyone else on the inner level. All are of equal value when the Real Self is taken into account. The physical body and personality are only a temporary abode for the Real Self.

CHAPTER 6

WHY ARE WE HERE?

Why are we here? I have been asking this question for years. Life, as I observed it going on around me as I grew up in England, appeared to make no sense at all. There were so many contradictions. People would say one thing, but their actions belied their words so often that I did not know which to believe—words or actions.

My parents were active members of the Church of England, and we regularly attended church. The vicar would preach an inspiring sermon each Sunday and the congregation *en masse* would assume a holy expression, as if each one had suddenly grown the wings of an angel. However, during the rest of the week these erstwhile angels dropped their masks and their habitual personalities were once more revealed. They acted in a very different way from the message of the sermon they so attentively listened to on the preceding Sunday. I was particularly astonished to watch the negative reactions that would erupt between various members at church meetings and in daily social contacts. Did anyone really practice Christ's teachings, I often wondered?

The next question that arose to confront me was whether I, myself, practiced Christ's teachings. The answer was regrettably in the negative. It was then, from my child's perspective, that I decided that only Jesus, who said he was the son of God, was capable of living fully according to the precepts he taught. But I, who was only a little girl, could not be expected to be as perfect as Jesus.

The fact that Jesus also taught that He and His Father were one was never explained, and when I dared to ask for an explanation, I was told that it was one of the mysteries, and must therefore remain as such and never be questioned, especially by a mere child and a presumptuous one at that. Never was I presented with the message which Baba, among many other world teachers, espouses, that each one of us is, in reality, God. To dare to suggest such a concept would have amounted to sacrilege and would have been severely punished.

So, sad to say, I turned away from the teachings as conveyed by the Christian Church. To me they were untrue and impractical, and the belief, as exemplified by the members, was hypocritical. I was disillusioned, helpless, and completely unable to live as the teachings directed. Jesus was also quoted as saying, "Of myself I can do nothing except the Father within me doeth the works," but that, too, was never explained to me.

The true meaning of the teachings that has so often been suppressed, is that we all, at the core of our being, are also God. A gradual, step-by-step process needs to be undertaken by which the many false layers that obscure the inner Reality can be removed. In this way, eventually, the God-Self can become fully visible and free to act as Master Puppeteer, animating the personality as a puppet, a musical instrument, or some other means through which to express Itself.

Many of the world teachers have, for centuries, taught that our essential being (or essence) can be likened to light or love. A common symbol that is frequently used to help with visualization is a light bulb or candle flame.

Baba tells us that he is God, but that we must also begin to realize that we, too, are God and that the only difference is that he is fully aware of his true identity, whereas we have forgotten who we really are.

If "God" can be identified with love, which is also our Real Self, then why are we not expressing love in our daily lives? Why has the heart by-pass occurred and how can it be reversed?

We need to take a deep look at our behavior to determine how, when, and under what circumstances we are by-passing our heart and ignoring our God-Self. Surely we are here on Earth to learn our true identity and allow It to live through us.

Baba teaches that everything that is not this Reality is excess luggage which we carry with us from past lives as well as this present one. One of his sayings expresses this idea succinctly:

> Reduce the luggage you carry about when on the journey of life. Remember that all that is not *you* is luggage! You are not the body, so the body is an item of luggage. The mind, the senses, the intelligence, the imagination, the desires, the plans, the prejudices, the discontent, the distress–all are items of luggage.
>
> Jettison them soon, to make travel lighter, safer and more comfortable. Learn this lesson by watching the great who are all humble and simple. They are the elders whom you should admire and follow. They are the people who bring forth your tears when they pass away; there are others who bring forth your tears when they pass your way! They are to be avoided.[1]

The Hi C (or Higher Consciousness) is constant and does not vary, so the numerous names by which people refer to It do not change Its identity. The numerous names act as symbols that different people can use to make closer contact with It. Exactly the same effect is in operation whether we choose to personify It as Christ, Mother Mary, Buddha, Sai Baba, or any other numinous personality. The chosen name or form makes no difference, for It is the same inner spark that exists within everyone. It expresses Itself as pure wisdom and love whenever the ego, with its multiple desires, is by-passed. If only more people could accept this truth! If we could cease the wasteful practice of acting as if only our particular form of belief and our preferred name and symbol are correct, the people of the world could finally be at peace with one another.

---

[1] Sai Baba, Sanathana Sarathi, June 1989.

We would not need to wage wars over who is right and who has the Truth, and who is wrong and who will be condemned to Hell.

There is only one God, Baba tells us, and God is love—not the hate which is so often expressed by various religious groups, all of whom believe they are the only so-called chosen ones. Children, when they are still quite young, know this to be true. They carry this knowledge from birth, when they are still close to the Source, until they are weaned away by other influences.

CHAPTER 7

The Four Functions in
Relation to the Heart By-Pass

The four functions—Intuition, Intellect, Sensation and Emotion—determine our behavior to a large extent, and in turn, our behavior affects our relationships. The four functions have a dual impact. They can be likened to windows through which we view the outer world and everyone and everything in it. They are also tools we can use to handle life in relation to other people, as well as in all the varied situations and experiences that are encountered throughout life. These functions determine how we react, depending on which ones are weak and barely conscious, or strong and available for use.

These functions have been gradually developing as we have evolved over many centuries. Sensation, which is shared by all living creatures, is the most basic and is essential for the survival and continuation of the species. The five senses (sight, hearing, smell, taste, and touch) act as guides. They alert all creatures to possible danger. The eyes indicate whether a path about to be taken is safe, that nothing in the landscape appears to be threatening, and that those they meet, whether animal or human, appear to be friendly. The eyes also allow choice, either to proceed, if what they see is pleasing, or to retreat if the opposite appears to be the case.

The ears bring attention to sounds that can be judged as safe and pleasing, and likely to lead to desirable experiences, or they can alert us to sounds that warn us of danger. Likewise, the nose and tongue help us decide what is safe, as well as what is pleasurable to eat and drink. In addition, the nose alerts both animals and people to the approach of an animal or a human being, so we can decide whether to continue on the way, or flee if it is perceived that there is possible danger ahead.

The skin, with its sense of touch, indicates if it is safe to walk in a certain direction, or if there are dangers of some sort that would be best avoided. The sense of touch also brings to our attention changes in temperature and air pressure.

With the aid of the senses, all living forms learn how to adapt to the environment. We need our five senses. They are essential as servants, but make unsatisfactory masters when in control of the host. If the sensation function were the only one available, we would all live at the level of the animals with whom we have this function in common.

The function of emotion or feeling allows a relationship with others of its kind. This can be either negative and aggressive, or positive and accepting. In its basic form, it, too, is shared with other species, but it is limited primarily to the immediate family and the group to which it belongs. It is expressed in the nurturing of the mother for the young, the attraction during mating, and the grooming and fondling with other members of the family. In human beings, emotion can be expanded to include many others outside the immediate family circle.

The intellect, the most recent function to become conscious, is the one that most often blocks the expression of love and caring. Many people whose intellect is strongly developed will try to express feelings and love through the thinking function and then wonder why the recipient is not appreciative of their expression. But no one can respond with gratitude to a cold way of expressing what can only be given through warmth and feeling.

Intuition can connect us directly to the Hi C to aid in the request for It to love through us.

In a relationship between two people, if both happen to have one or more of the same functions equally well-developed, they will usually communicate more easily than if they do not share a common strong function. They may think of it as being on the same wavelength, as distinct from being at cross purposes.

The generally uneven development of the four functions and the common lack of emotion, or the feeling function, is the root cause of the heart by-pass.

CHAPTER 8

PERSONAL RELATIONSHIPS

Many people believe that if the conditions in their lives were improved, and if all the people with whom they are in contact could be changed and were less difficult to handle, they would automatically be happier.

But not only do we have no authority even to try to change someone else, it is literally impossible to succeed in doing so, and only backfires onto those who attempt it. Surely, it is a sufficiently formidable task to try to change ourselves, yet that is precisely where we need to begin.

When we are willing to turn the spotlight onto our own behavior and begin to bring about the necessary changes, often, to our immense surprise, those people whom we have here-to-fore found to be difficult, suddenly and for no apparent reason, appear to us in a different light. When this happens, we think they have changed, but in reality, it is we who have gained a clearer perspective that enables us to react in a different way to them.

We all tend to react to outer stimuli from events and people. But what we invariably fail to realize is that while we are reacting to others, they are, at the same time, also reacting to us. Such interaction results in a vicious circle. The only way to break it is for one or the other, and preferably both of the participants, to stop reacting. We need to step back to observe the situation so that each person can concentrate on his or her own behavior with a view to remedying it.

Many of us have cherished expectations revolving around our acceptance by others. "Does this or that one like me?" we ask. "Am I popular? Do I have many friends?" We all want to be accepted, especially by our peers. But we tend to forget that our own attitude to others, to a greater or lesser degree, dictates their behavior toward us, and determines whether they like or dislike us. Whatever attitude we present to others, we will inevitably receive back from them, either consciously or unconsciously.

We all have some kind of a relationship with everyone in our lives, both in the present life as well as in previous incarnations. We have all had innumerable impersonal relationships. Each one of them can teach us something we need to learn about ourselves and about relating to other people. When we accept this idea, all relationships will be more meaningful, and we will begin to understand that it is no accident that certain people are in our lives.

As I look back over my long life at the many different kinds of relationships it has contained, I have to admit that some of the most difficult ones have proved in the long run to have been the most productive in my personal development.

My mother is a prime example, though I would never have admitted that while I was growing up under her severe control. Even now I am surprised that I am willing to express it! As I look back I realized that I learned at least two important lessons: primarily, I learned how painful the control she wielded can be to another person and particularly to a child; secondly, I was forced to withdraw within myself to find security.

Since I became involved in the reverie work and learned about some of my past lives, I have begun to realize that in my mother I was meeting a former facet of myself who was a very controlling type of person. I had to experience in this present life the pain and feelings of impotence I used to cause others. What better way to learn that lesson?

In an interview with Sai Baba he once told me that this present life could teach me much more than a life as a sadhak or renunciate. It could teach me patience, tolerance, steadfastness, and forbearance!

True and meaningful relationships involve clear and honest communication flowing freely between two people. I have worked with many people, and over the years I've learned that effective communication is one of the most difficult of all activities to practice, and for some people, it is impossible to achieve.

It is all too common for people to interact with one another primarily on a very shallow and superficial level between the persona, mask, or role, rather than relating to the whole personality.

Chapter 9

PARTNERS

Sai Baba says that the interaction between individuals who live together in a close daily relationship, such as marriage, can be likened to the way two rough stones shaken together in a jar will each polish the rough surfaces of the other by the friction resulting from being rubbed against one another. This polishing process can, if accepted, give each partner the chance to work off old karmic patterns and learn the lessons that still need to be completed.

This is by no means always a pleasant situation, and many people prefer to withdraw from the interaction if it is too stressful, and seek another partner with whom they hope their shared life will be more harmonious. However, this decision invariably results in a new relationship which may be free from the former problems, but complete with a new set, designed either to rub off other rough edges from each of the new partners, or even the same ones as before, replete with the same challenges they had tried to escape in the former partnership.

If the interaction is accepted, together with the frictions, it is possible, with the aid of a partner, to learn and grow into a more mature and whole person even more rapidly and on a deeper level than is possible alone.

As this basic connection between two adults directly affects their children and succeeding generations, it is most important to try to discover why it so often fails.

Baba advises us to visualize within each person the hidden or unseen divinity, which he says can be likened to a flame covered over by an outer shell comprised of the body with its senses, the mind which he often refers to as a monkey mind, the personality, and the ego. This outer visible part is usually what we judge as pleasing or unpleasant when we try to communicate or develop a relationship with someone.

Most people are self-involved and too busy to stop for even a moment to re-focus and break the habit of reacting to the more obvious personality of another person. But not until we can do so can we start to call forth the inner Reality both from within ourselves as well as from inside everyone else.

It is particularly important for two people living together in a shared experience to honor the divinity within each other, or they will discover that their relationship, which started out on such a positive note, has, to their consternation and for no foreseen reason, begun to deteriorate.

In my book, *Cutting More Ties that Bind*, I advocate the use of the Triangle Exercise to help two people in a close relationship to consult the inner Mentor (or Hi C or Higher Consciousness) for guidance. As is outlined in other parts of the same book, all the different roles people play in various areas of their lives must be dropped before a close connection between the two real parts of a couple is possible. Then it becomes, "Thy will, not mine be done," the "thy" referring to the Hi C of each one, instead of the more usual situation where one or the other partner insists that what he or she wants be accepted by the other. If this method or some other equally appropriate one is resorted to, it is possible for a solution to problems to be forthcoming which will insure the best interests of each partner. That inner part of each of us really does know what is best for us even though we may find it hard to accept this concept. We all tend to think that we know what is good for us, but experience eventually proves that this is far from the truth, as exemplified by the sorry plight of so many people with good intentions but an inability to make wise decisions in their lives.

Another essential ingredient for a successful relationship is for the heart of each partner to be kept open to the other. This means that each one needs to listen to the other with full attention and with a caring attitude, without the critical mind of either one getting in the way.

I find this to be extremely important today, for it is often necessary for both partners to work outside the home in order to maintain their standard of living. In this case, the role each needs to play in the workplace must be discarded as soon as they both arrive home, where work roles are not appropriate for their life together. So many times I have heard the complaint that a partner continues to be a doctor, teacher, lawyer, actor, business executive, or some other role dictated by their occupation, after leaving the work place and returning home. When this is true of both people, then the roles each has assumed at work will be relating to one another instead of the people who assume the roles. The results are doomed from the start, as there will be no common language.

From my experience gleaned from working with many different types of men and women from varied backgrounds and national groups, I have come to the conclusion that the most serious and widespread problem is a lack of communication. In many cases an actual inability to communicate exists between individuals, which in turn causes serious problems between groups, organizations, and nations.

Far too often, each participant in a proposed discussion is only interested in presenting his or her point of view. There is little or no interest in hearing what the other person has to contribute, especially if it appears that it may be contrary to a cherished opinion. Very often conversations are reduced to an ego trip, with each speaker enjoying hearing his or her own voice, with very little consideration for the effect of the words on the listener. This lack is an example of too much Yang energy in operation and too little Yin. In other words, each person is exerting more energy and interest in assertive thinking and talking, and too little to receptive listening and feeling. Talking is a Yang (or assertive) activity, usually under the control of the brain, while listening is Yin (or receptive), and connected to the heart.

It is patently obvious that this imbalance is one of the main causes of the world heart by-pass.

A vast majority of people do not know how to listen. Instead, they tend to concentrate on whatever they wish to say themselves, and they wait impatiently for the other person to stop talking long enough for them to speak, or even go so far as to interrupt one another in their eagerness to be heard.

This behavior pattern is usually the result of early experiences with one or both parents. Many children and young people with whom I work tell me with deep disappointment that they were never granted the privilege of having a parent really listen to them, and that communication was usually one-sided, with the parent doing most of the talking at them instead of with them.

I have observed in my counselling work that just being willing to listen to people with full and undivided attention is often sufficient to enable them to see more clearly what needs to be done in a particular situation, or with a newly perceived aspect of themselves that needs their attention. To be able to act as a caring sounding board is often exactly what confused or anxious people most need and may never have experienced before. One woman expressed it aptly by saying that she was grateful for a *loving ear.*

However, communication cannot be one-sided. We all need to be able to alternate by sometimes being the one who talks while the other listens, and at other times the reverse. In this way, each partner practices balancing the Yin and Yang energy which is essential for overall health.

The listener needs to be as impersonal as possible, with no criticism or judgment of the one speaking. It is also preferable if the listener is able to keep in mind that only the ego can be hurt, not the Real Self, and that everything someone else says is merely that person's opinion, reaction, or projection and is not necessarily always the truth.

However, it is important for each partner to be open to consider any complaints or criticisms as a signal to determine whether the complaints are valid and if they do apply personally, or if they are projections of the other person's problems. Much benefit can be derived from such an exchange if it brings to one partner's attention something about himself or herself that needs to be changed or worked through.

It is also helpful if the listener can remember to remove personal beliefs or thoughts and really concentrate on listening to what the partner has to say. Otherwise, it is a great temptation to hear only what one wants to hear or what is in line with one's own ideas, and to blank out what is being said if one does not want to hear it or deal with it later.

Some couples still have difficulty in communicating, in spite of an attempt to use the above suggestions. This is especially the case if one partner finds it easier to talk than the other who may have difficulty in expressing himself or herself. In addition, the "quiet partner" may feel overwhelmed by the barrage of words from the talkative one.

To make it easier for communication to take place, the Catholic church initiated a program offering an alternate method in such situations. During a weekend retreat, it is suggested to the couples who attend that it might be easier if each partner would write out as simply and clearly as possible, and preferably without implied criticism of the other, whatever he or she would like to express. Each partner is more relaxed and can more easily collect his or her thoughts when not actually facing and interacting with the other.

When each one has finished writing, he or she is asked to exchange with one another what has been written. It is also suggested that each partner can go to a quiet place to be alone to read each other's written material.

Communication, to be successful, should be a two-way activity, in which two people undertake to exchange ideas on a given subject for their mutual benefit.

I find that men will write primarily from their heads, as they are usually more Yang, assertive, and factual in their outlook, and like to present what they think about a situation or relationship. Women, on the other hand, usually prefer to state how they feel, which is more Yin, receptive, and intuitive. However, there are variations on this attitude that originate from early training. Another exception to this concept occurs if either or both of the individuals have developed the opposite aspect of themselves and are able both to think and feel. But it is more often a case of "the twain shall never meet."

Only when each one is willing to listen to the other, as well as expressing ideas and feelings, can true communication take place. If men only think and plan what appears to be logical and practical, with no concern for the effect on others, and if women only use feeling to determine what will benefit others, without the logical approach involving how to proceed, there can be no solution to this overwhelming problem at the personal as well as at the universal level.

In a mixed group that includes both men and women, their very different ways of communication, as well as their differing viewpoints and the things that are important to them, become increasingly apparent.

Men tend to indulge in words and more words, weaving a veritable web in the mistaken belief that they are communicating. But unless the message is understood and accepted by the listener, they may just as well save the breath, time, and energy of them both. Women are also prone to an ego trip, but they are usually more interested in how a certain proposed plan will effect everyone who will participate in its fulfillment. Their approach is more from a feeling level.

In my work, I advocate the use of a symbol called the mandala, which depicts the four functions we all have at our disposal in different degrees of development. The functions that are dominant need to be toned down, and the weak ones (or less conscious ones) need to be brought up from the unconscious where they have lain dormant, and consciously exercised until they are available and can be reliably utilized.

However, this practice is not always a pleasant undertaking. We all prefer to rely on our strong functions or abilities because they bring us success, whereas those that are underdeveloped are often the cause of our failures. It is important to have all four functions at our disposal if we are to live fulfilling and successful lives.

We all know how painful it is to engage in a physical exercise that requires us to develop any muscles that we do not habitually use. At first they are very painful from the unaccustomed use, but if we persist long enough, they become less painful until we are able to use them as easily and painlessly as we do all the others. The same applies to our nonphysical muscles. If we persevere in using our less conscious or weaker functions, we will probably undergo an initial period when we make mistakes and possibly meet with failure. But, as with other types of exercise, our performance will improve with practice, and we will benefit from the additional abilities that allow us to be well-rounded individuals instead of lopsided ones.

Chapter 10

The Heart By-Pass in the Family and Home

In a great number of families, especially in our society, the members show more of the negative than the positive side of their personalities to one another. They can be the life of the party, a Mother Teresa, a Prince Charming, or an angel to friends and acquaintances, but at home in the so-called bosom of the family, they often act very differently. One of the common excuses for such contrasting behavior is that they have to "put up a good front" or present their "public image" when out in the world, but at home they can "let down their hair" and be themselves.

But "Charity should start at home," as the old saying would have it, for the members of our family are usually the very ones who offer us the best opportunity to work out our karma, so they can be valuable teachers.

Childhood is a time when patterns of behavior are established which can affect our whole lives. As all young creatures learn by example, by actions rather than words, the way the parents interact with one another sets the pattern for their children's future relationships.

Baba has a favorite saying, "You cannot always oblige, but you should always speak and act obligingly." This certainly applies to the way we behave to one another in the family. The home should be a training ground where family members can learn to act in a loving way with each other and thus pave the way to more caring behavior to others.

Babies are not born complete with all they need to know to live in a fulfilling way. They have a certain potential, but they need to be taught by having that potential encouraged and developed. If this is accomplished, they will go out from the home and into the world well-equipped to form their own loving nucleus which will then attract other like-minded and loving people to them. In this way a more caring approach to life will filter out into society to rekindle the dormant essence within each of those it touches.

Usually, "family" refers to the immediate unit consisting of two parents and their children, but it actually includes the extended family, comprising grandparents and other close relatives of both husband and wife.

Many jokes involve in-laws, especially mothers-in-law, but both sides of a family need to be considered and given appropriate attention. However, that does not imply that they should be allowed unlimited control. It merely means treating them with respect, yet remaining firm if and when they try to take over and impose their demands if these are unreasonable.

I frequently hear complaints about a husband's or wife's family and sometimes a person will remark with bitterness, "I thought I was marrying my partner, but I actually feel I have married the whole family." This unfortunate situation is not as likely to be a problem when both partners have cut the ties to each of their parents in the puberty ritual before the marriage takes place.[1]

Practical boundaries are essential and should be made clear from the very beginning. This helps avoid resentment from building up and festering because it was unexpressed by either partner. Again, Baba's injunction applies, "You cannot always oblige, but you should always speak and act obligingly." This attitude will lay down a positive pattern for children to follow later in their lives when they are faced with similar situations.

We cannot take responsibility for anyone else's behavior, but we are free to choose how we react, whether from anger which stems from insecurity, or by silently requesting the Hi C to act and speak through us. Only the personality and ego can be hurt, ridiculed, or embarrassed. The Real Self is immune as It is secure in Its own worth which is neither more nor less than anyone else's.

---

[1] See page 42 for more discussion of this idea.

With the ever-increasing incidence of divorce and separation, in addition to the relatives of the two parents, the extended family becomes quite complicated. When the mother or father remarries, or is dating someone else, the families of the new partners will be included. This situation is difficult, at best, for all concerned. It is especially hard for the children of the various families who have to adjust to a step-mother, a step-father and sometimes both, as well as other members of the new family in addition to their own parents.

Under such circumstances the same guidelines can be applied as those suggested for the treatment of in-laws. Such an attitude may not result in an immediate miracle where everyone lives "happily ever after" as promised by the fairy tales, but it can alleviate some of the internal stress, particularly for the children.

If we accept the concept that everyone and everything in our lives can be used to teach us valuable lessons, and we can also rear our children to ask what they need to learn from the various relationships, they can greatly benefit from them instead of becoming angry and resentful.

CHAPTER 11

REVIVING THE PUBERTY RITES

In the reverie in which Baba introduced me to the heart by-pass, he explained only too clearly that the global heart by-pass has its roots far back in history. It has been so rapidly increasing ever since, that in recent times its effect is clearly perceptible both in individuals, organizations, and groups in every country throughout the world. We cannot change the past. It is gone forever. But we can change the future by our own actions day by day.

We need to find a way to stop this paralyzing process, whereby more and more people are cutting off the flow of love from their hearts, and endeavoring to live primarily with their brains and bodies. We can be responsible only for ourselves and our own actions, and only in the present. That means giving our full attention to the changes that need to take place in each of us, instead of indulging in the common practice of criticizing others for their shortcomings and ignoring our own.

To break the chain reaction of the heart by-pass from earliest times until the present, we must discover ways to reverse this ongoing process in ourselves now, before it becomes even more overwhelming and controlling at the world level.

It must start with a different way of educating children. Before that can begin, the parents who are responsible for the early training of their children will need to detach themselves from the effects of their own childhood conditioning, which inexorably has led to the present heartless situation in which we all exist.

In all the old cultures, and in some scattered present-day ones, various types of puberty rituals were designed to mark the passage from childhood to maturity. Remnants of these practices can still be detected in the Jewish Bar Mitzvah, Confirmation in the Christian church, and similar rites in other religions. But the deep significance of such rituals has been lost, or is so diluted in meaning that they are rarely fully understood by the young participants.

During these old rituals, young girls and boys were removed physically from under the care of the parents, and taken from the secure nest their home had provided during their childhood years. The practice had a similar effect as that achieved by parents of all species who push their young out into the world as soon as they are deemed capable of fending for themselves.

But for human children, the ritual has an additional significance. Children pass naturally through specific stages in the growth process from birth to puberty. They start out as helpless infants completely dependent upon adults for their care and security. They react in whatever way they perceive will bring them necessary attention from their parents and other members of the family. They will scream if they discern that to be the only way they can gain attention, or coo and smile if such behavior assures them of their needs being met, for the most primitive of all the instincts is that of self-preservation and survival.

At this early stage children are completely self-involved and intent only on using any means they discover to be successful in procuring what they need to survive. At puberty, when they are growing beyond childhood into adolescence and approaching adulthood, they have to be taught how to take responsibility for their own needs. In addition, young adults are expected to be capable of taking their place as responsible members of the group of which they are a part. Children used to be removed from the parental nest where all their needs were met and where they were concerned only with themselves and what they wanted. They could then be taught by the elders of the group the basic requirements to become active members of the extended family. In this way they moved out of "me-oriented" behavior to the next phase which involves others and their needs, and thence the needs of the group as a whole.

Unfortunately, because this custom has been neglected for so long, many people fail to make the vital transition from pre-puberty "me-based" behavior to the more mature "we" concept that is essential to keep the heart open and the love flowing out to others. Young adults are often stuck in their emotional development and cannot move into true maturity. In the work I have been taught, a simple puberty ritual to revive this important step has been made available for use at this present time. It is called "Cutting the Ties that Bind," and has been presented in the book of that title.

Of course, the appropriate time for this ritual is about the age of puberty. However, it is effective at whatever age it is undertaken, though it obviously takes longer to remove the overlay of many years if it is delayed too long. But it has become apparent that this ritual greatly assists in the reversal of the heart by-pass, as it successfully enables people to move beyond the stage where so many seem to be trapped. Concern and caring for others can be activated at any age.

When people have cut the ties from both parents, they are free to move beyond the stage of self-interest and self-love to a more mature and unselfish level of being able to give love and to receive it. This ability appears to be sadly lacking in many relationships that are based mainly on physical, sexual, or mental attraction. When, with time, the initial stimulation abates, if the love for one another which could cement the union is not active, the two people drift apart, each going off in search of a new partner with whom they hope to enjoy a more lasting relationship. The increased incidence of divorce or separation is a direct result of an inability to move beyond the self-gratification of childhood to the ability to love another in a caring way by being open to the other's welfare rather than only to one's own wishes.

When two people form a partnership where love and caring flows freely, they will be well-prepared to become equally loving parents. They don't need to repeat with their own children the same treatment they received from their parents. Even though adults remember the lack of love they experienced as children, they often unconsciously treat their own children in the same way, forgetting how it felt. When prospective parents are guided through the puberty ritual, at whatever age, they can more easily assume the role of parenthood and move from self-interest and self-love to the unselfish attitude required of an adult, and particularly of a parent.

They can then, in turn, make sure that their children are gradually taught simple steps toward unselfishness by starting to reach out to others. As the children approach puberty, they will be willing to share. In this way, these young adults can move from self-interest to the more expansive love that is possible for an adult. Then, when they, too, have acquired independence from their parents and are free to express their individual qualities, they can, with the aid of a partner, create a stable foundation suitable for raising a family. Under such circumstances the heart by-pass can be reversed and the children can be trained to balance their Yin and Yang energies.

However, few people are prepared in this way, with the unfortunate result that many families lack the kind of love that frees the various members to be dependent on the Real Self instead of on other people, or on one another.

We are all born into an already existing family with a long ancestral line that stretches back in time from both parents. We also inherit all the relatives on both sides, each of whom can become one of our teachers to help us learn from our interaction with them.

This original family unit is, therefore, our first classroom, where we are given an opportunity to learn the basic lessons. It should also be where we practice treating family members with consideration for their welfare. Most of us would probably hesitate to shout or behave in a rude or angry or impatient manner to strangers, yet we frequently expose our own family to our worst behavior and think nothing of insulting, accusing, criticizing, or deprecating our parents, partners, children, siblings, and other relatives. The usual excuse is that we need to relax when we are at home.

The heart by-pass starts with us, so we are the only ones who can reverse it. The perfect place to start is at home with the very people who are best suited to be our teachers. Instead of taking them for granted because we think of them as possessions, and treating them in whatever way we may choose according to our own desires, we can start to open up our hearts and let the love from the Hi C flow through us to each of them. In this way, many personality clashes will be prevented, and each person will be given a chance to reverse the heart by-pass in the personal family arena.

When viewed in this way, this appears to be a vast undertaking. It most certainly is if we look at the entire world with all the negativity and lack of love so visible everywhere. We are responsible for our own small part, and if we concentrate on our behavior, first with those who are close to us in the family, we will be joining forces with others intent on the same practice, and in this way the world will begin to change. The world is made up of millions of individuals. As we reverse the heart by-pass in our own lives, it is obvious that many small sections will begin to change. We do not need to worry about the large picture. We are responsible only for our own small part. So what are we all waiting for? Is it so hard to allow the Hi C to use us to send them love?

It worked with the hi-jackers, who were professional hate-mongers, so surely it will do as well, if not a great deal better, for the people with whom we spend so much of our time and energy.

CHAPTER 12

PARENTS WHO CAUSE A BY-PASS
of THEIR CHILDREN'S HEARTS

I can still remember a very controversial book that was written in 1942. The title was *A Generation of Vipers* by Phillip Wiley.[1] At the time it made a big impression on me, and since then I have observed how correct some of Wiley's conclusions were at that time, and still are now. He coined a new word, *Momism*, to describe the way so many mothers spoil their sons in the mistaken belief that this is an expression of love. But, actually the exact opposite is true, as it is a very subtle form of control. The mother keeps her son trapped in a childish dependency upon her, attached to her and her praise and indulgence, which renders him helpless to break free and move beyond childhood.

These *puers eternis*, or eternal boys, often take one of two possible directions in their adult lives. In some cases they choose the homosexual way, and are attracted to reflections of themselves which other men mirror for them. The other path is the Don Juan role of having multiple sexual relationships that don't last. They remain at a pre-adult stage, where they are unable to make the break from the mother and move into adulthood, beyond the stage of being in love with themselves. Some of these men make an enormous effort to try to overcome this imbalance, and bridge the gap in their development by assuming a macho manner and over-achieving in some pursuit.

---

[1] Phillip Wiley, *A Generation of Vipers* (New York: Rinehart & Company, 1942, 1955).

The eternal child in such men is often quite enchanting, and appeals to the maternal impulse in a woman, but after a while it palls, for only rarely do most women want to be a mother to their husbands or lovers. If they marry, and the wife gets pregnant, these men often become very threatened. When the baby arrives, they can be extremely jealous and resent the fact that the wife is giving more of her attention to the baby and less to them. In some cases, these men will leave at the onset of the pregnancy, and search for a woman who will devote all of her attention to them and their needs. But as soon as the pattern repeats itself, they will leave again in search of another victim.

It is not only men who have been kept at a pre-adult stage. Some fathers follow a similar behavior pattern when they keep their daughters dependent on them indefinitely. This prolonged bond reminds me of a popular song introduced by Mary Martin many years ago, "My Heart Belongs to Daddy."

When either parent reigns supreme in an adult child's heart, there is no room left for a mate to occupy it. So, future relationships are likely to be shallow and self-serving, or numerous and of short duration. In either event, love and caring are usually absent.

When the ties are cut from both parents, and the boy or girl is taught how to live as an independent adult in the community, a future partnership with someone who has also passed over into true maturity is possible and fulfilling. Then each one is able to consider the welfare of the various members of the family and not only what each of them wants.

As more families learn to live in such a responsible way, they will have an impact in their own social circle, which, in turn, can bring about changes in the society where they live and eventually reach even further afield.

It is an interesting fact that those people who are the least sensitive to the feelings of others are often supersensitive when their own feelings are involved, especially if they sense the slightest hint of criticism, even when none was intended. It is part of the extreme self-involvement that so often accompanies a blocked heart.

People who have been abused in childhood tend to repeat that same pattern with their own children. I first became aware of this tendency when working with children of parents who were survivors of Nazi concentration camps. It was hard for me to believe that when these young people married and had children they would often treat them as they themselves had been treated in the camp. Apparently, having been help-lessly at the mercy of their jailers, they would vent their frus-tration and anger onto their children who were even more helpless, as if that somehow made up for not being able to fight back when they had been abused in the camp. This nega-tive behavior pattern seems to have been imprinted so deeply that they needed to externalize it to try to exorcise it. But to attempt to do so in that way merely continued a chain reac-tion.

CHAPTER 13

Child Abuse—Sexual and Otherwise

Child abuse, and in particular, sexual abuse of children, has become far more apparent than has been the case until the present time. It has finally emerged from undercover where it has been hidden out of sight and acknowledgment, usually due to the threats of the perpetrators to the molested children that they would suffer dire consequences if they ever told anyone about the abuse they suffered.

Children instinctively look up to adults as authority figures, and accept whatever adults tell them as the truth. In addition, adults are so much older, bigger, and more powerful than children, that the latter fear that if they disobey they will indeed suffer at the hands of their abusers in even more frightening ways. So they usually remain silent, and often suppress even the memory or consciousness of the assault, especially if it took place when they were very young. However, the effect of the abuse remains with them, but at a deep unconscious level, and it has a negative affect on all subsequent relationships.

If the abuser was the father, it often happens that, even when the mother was aware of the situation, she was afraid to confront her husband for fear of his anger and possible attack on her, so she remained silent. In addition, she may have been jealous that her husband was involved in such an intimate relationship with their daughter, which she may even view as rejection of herself. When this is the case, she will blame the daughter for inciting the father. She may feel the daughter is in competition with herself for the father's attention. Even when the husband has turned to the daughter in this way because his relationship with his wife had become unsatisfactory, the mother will usually throw the blame on the daughter rather than examining the relationship with her husband to attempt to improve it. In that case, the child cannot trust either parent, and will continue to carry over this mistrust and project it onto future relationships with all the attendant heartache.

Some young girls who have been sexually abused by a parent or other relative, friend of the family, or stranger, feel so much guilt over the experience that they become promiscuous in a desperate attempt to punish themselves for what they instinctively realize is a tabu. Or they continue to practice a pattern of behavior introduced to them through the abuse.

Again, such abuse presents an extreme example of the heart being closed off to the effect that personal desire for self-gratification has on others. It is an even more serious offense when a child–who is not in a position to protest or refuse to participate–is the victim.

Many incidents of physical abuse of children have different causes. When parents are too young and lack experience, or have been mistreated by their own parents, they will vent their anger or frustration on anyone who is weaker, younger, or unable to resist, which is often their own children. This is particularly the case if they have been led to believe that they own their children instead of only borrowing them for this life experience.

Another horrifying practice that has come to light recently involves the sexual abuse of children in poor countries by men who use these defenseless victims in any way they please, often with the cooperation of the children's parents, who even sell their children for the money they need to survive.

Baba teaches that we are all one, so we should treat each person as God. This means that whatever we do to others we actually do to ourselves, since we are all one at the core of our being.

Surely this fact alone should be sufficient to persuade each of us to stop, look, and listen to what we are thinking, feeling, saying, and doing to hurt others, for it will eventually boomerang and hurt us.

CHAPTER 14

Competitiveness and the Heart By-Pass

I have been taught in the reverie work that the only person in the entire world with whom it is realistic to compete is oneself. Each of us is at a certain stage on our inner return journey back to the Real self. No two people are at the same place at the same time, or even on an identical path. Therefore, either to compete with anyone else or compare ourselves with others is useless, and a sheer waste of time and energy. To do so would be like trying to compare two runners, each starting at a different place at a different time and moving in different directions toward an individual goal, yet trying to compete with one another. Expressed in this way, such competition is obviously impossible. Yet, that is the foolish practice that so many people attempt by competing or comparing themselves with others. This useless comparison always ends in failure and frustration.

The only realistic attitude to everything that happens in life (and everyone we meet, or with whom we have a close contact) is to ask what challenge or opportunity it presents as a test in the "school of life" to help us determine what we have really learned. In other words, everything with which we are faced is like a measuring stick to show us where we are in the learning process. Considered from this position, whatever other people's lives contain, both outer possessions and inner faults, attributes, or abilities, should not concern us. They are for their learning, not our's. However, we can observe them, and in that way we can learn from them by looking at them as if in a mirror. Only when we recognize our own failings through interaction with others can we work on them.

Comparison with others can be helpful if we allow it to stimulate us to attend to our own life, or if it shows us an example of what is possible to achieve if we let the Hi C use us as Its instrument.

The more we try to compete with others in order to beat them, or overpower them, the more we are contributing to our own heart by-pass, and consequently to the larger global loveless situation. When we endeavor to set our own life in order and let the Hi C live and act through us, we can also allow It to use each of us to direct Its love to others. This will automatically result in our own hearts being opened.

It is saddening to observe the effects on young children, even in kindergarten, who are being more and more infected by the need to compete with others instead of exercising their own muscles, both physical and mental, to succeed in their own development. Education is becoming increasingly a matter of learning in order to beat others, to reach the top and reap rewards.

Competitiveness is extremely damaging when children are encouraged to compete with their siblings. Each child is born into a—family as if magnetically attracted to it—by its own requirements to learn certain lessons and thus work out karmic debts that need to be balanced or eliminated. Since each child has a different series of past incarnations, it is confusing to be faced with the unequal task of competing with siblings who are older or younger and who need a different challenge.

Too many children are compared with brothers and sisters in a vain attempt to persuade one child to succeed in some area where he or she appears to be lacking in qualities or abilities where the others have no such problems. If a lack is so severe that the child fails to compete successfully with a more accomplished sibling, the child may feel so hopeless that he or she will give up and cease trying to learn.

It is not easy, especially in the increasingly hectic life we are all being forced to live, to find a way to help each child discover the qualities that still need to be developed. Unfortunately, the strong patterns brought in from generation to generation create habits that become automatic reactions, and parents who have been forced to compete with their own siblings will, in turn, often treat their children in the same way, despite the fact that the parents may have suffered from such treatment themselves when they were children.

Chapter 15

The Heart By-Pass in the Work Place

In this present day and age, the majority of men and women are employed daily in some type of occupation outside the home. It has become increasingly difficult for a couple to live comfortably and to raise a family on one salary, so the two-income family is fast becoming the normal mode. This situation often creates a great strain on all the family members, and the working mother is especially stressed. As a rule, in addition to her job, she is also responsible for all the usual chores attendant on running a household, as well as her dual roles as wife and mother. Gradually, working parents are achieving a balance because more fathers are willing to assume some of the work connected to the home and the children. As sharing the workload is more generally accepted, some of the burden will be removed from working mothers.

When both parents are under abnormal stress, all members of the family are bound to be affected by it. The inevitable result of this widespread problem prevents them from opening their hearts, so the love which could ease the tension is rarely expressed in a complete and satisfying manner.

However, each person is being given an opportunity to be used in the work place and in the home to provide a nucleus which can then spread to those who share the same space and eventually spill over into the community in which they live and work.

Stress has become a catch-word which is used to describe a wide variety of adverse reactions to many different experiences. It can be cited as an excuse for avoiding anything that is not to someone's liking. If we do not want to do something, it is convenient to refuse by saying that we are under too much stress to be able to comply. In more extreme cases of avoidance, it is an excuse for laziness.

But what exactly is stress? In the reverie work, I have been taught that the main cause of stress is resistance to something or someone, and the nervousness that accompanies such a reaction.

I recall the wise doctor who helped deliver my younger daughter by the natural childbirth method that was first introduced by an English doctor named Grantly Dick Read. During the prenatal meetings with him, he explained that pain during childbirth is usually caused by tension and resistance to the contractions. If the mother can relax and use her breathing to help the process, she will feel far less pain during the birth process. Both mother and baby can then benefit from a much easier and less painful delivery.

Many athletes have also found that when they relax during competition they will be less tense and tired after such physical exertion. There have been accounts of those who have practiced letting go and moving to a different level where they are animated from within. When this idea gained popularity with sports enthusiasts, several books were written outlining the theory, among them, *Inner Game of Tennis*[1] and others of a similar type.

One of my all-time favorite volumes is *Zen in the Art of Archery*, by Herrigel,[2] in which the author expounds the theory that if an archer waits in the position for shooting an arrow from his taut bow until the arrow is released *through* him instead of *by* him, it will hit the bull's eye without his will being involved and with no strain or effort being expended on his part.

In my own work, I meet many professional therapists, a large number of whom tell me that they go home after a

---

[1] W. Timothy Gallwey, *Inner Game of Tennis* (New York: Bantam Books, 1984).

[2] Eugene Herrigel, *Zen in the Art of Archery* (New York: Random, 1971).

day of counselling totally exhausted and carrying with them the problems of the various clients they have seen that day. Some of them have even informed me that they feel they are burning out and are considering changing their profession for one that is less demanding.

By using the method that has been given to me, I have learned that it is not necessary to feel exhausted at the end of a day's counselling, or to take the clients' problems home, which does not help either them or the therapist. When the therapist or facilitator surrenders to the Hi C, trusts It to supply the needed help, and accepts whatever It supplies, the entire experience is one of relaxed listening within whereby both the therapist and the patient are taught from the Hi C available to each of them. It has been proved to be true, not only for me, but for many who adopt this method. Many reports have reached me that not only do the sessions proceed in a more flowing manner, but instead of ending the day depleted of energy, the therapists find that they are more energized.

The field of therapy is just one of the many occupations about which complaints of stress are so common.

It is possible to experience the same absence of stress in all occupations if we can allow the Hi C to work though us rather than straining to accomplish the work with our own will. Then there is no excuse for being exhausted at the end of each day or to fear burnout. I always tell those who work in a therapy setting that if they feel depleted they are at fault for not working in the correct way. They could let the Hi C perform the job through them as Its instrument.

When just one person in a work place demonstrates the ability to be an instrument of the universal Hi C, and is also willing to direct the love from this inner source to all those with whom he or she comes in daily contact, changes must take place which will reach out into the world to help to reverse the global heart by-pass.

We do not have to love all of our co-workers. We do not even have to like them, but we can always direct the love from the Hi C to them which may open their hearts as well as our own. Many people have told me that when they are willing to

practice this simple little exercise daily, erstwhile difficult relationships have improved immeasurably, which they found
hard to believe after having suffered so long from their daily
aggravation. It is up to each of us. Are we willing to do our
small part to *re-connect* the heart or do we expect other people
to do it for us?

CHAPTER 16

THE HEART BY-PASS WITH SERVICE PEOPLE

One of the areas where the heart by-pass is particularly noticeable is with some people's interaction with those who offer various kinds of service.

It sometimes appears that all the frustration a person may have suffered at the hands of parents, partners, business associates, and especially bosses, is vented on those who are deemed to be inferior or less important. But these people are just as sensitive to insult, rejection, or inappropriate treatment as are those whom they serve and who treat them disrespectfully.

This tendency to take out frustration and anger on people who appear to be weaker or less fortunate is a common one. When people have been treated badly, instead of accepting the *karma* involved and learning how painful it is to be treated in that way, they invariably deliver the same kind of treatment to someone who is weaker, or younger, or who cannot defend himself or herself. This reaction apparently gives a sense of power that had been lost by having been unjustly treated themselves. But this sense of power is gained at the expense of the present victim. Those who give vent to this kind of retaliation will have to undergo similar treatment at the hands of someone else, either in this lifetime or in a future one. In this way the action and reaction is perpetuated in a vicious circle, which keeps many people pinned to the wheel of death and rebirth indefinitely. Taking out our frustrations on those who serve us merely hurts us in the long run, as we are bound to reap the rewards of our actions at some time by receiving the same treatment we gave out.

I have often observed people in a restaurant carrying on an animated conversation with a partner or a group of friends in a very pleasant fashion, all smiles and charm. When it is time to place the orders, their attitudes often change radically. These people become overly authoritative, talk down to the waiter, and treat him as an underling to show off their superiority. They flaunt their knowledge of the menu, and particularly of the wine list, to impress on their companions that they are aficionados. Or, men may choose a different approach if a woman is waiting on them. They may flirt with her to show their prowess with women, but with no consideration for the feelings either of the waitress or, for that matter, of their female companions.

Some people's treatment of shop assistants is equally demeaning. Their job, like that of a waiter or waitress, is very tiring, as they are on their feet all day, yet some people treat them as if they were slaves hired to do their bidding, like machines instead of human beings. Another example of the lack of consideration, or even of good manners, is the way some women treat hairdressers, who need the patience of Job to withstand the demands of some women, many of whom expect to be made to look like models when they have hair that is thin or damaged by too many bleaches.

It takes only a little thought, together with a caring approach, to bring lightness and humor instead of criticism and ingratitude into these people's lives. As we are willing to give, so will we receive. If we only concentrate on what someone will give us, we will find that they no longer are willing to fill our demands, or if they do, it will be done grudgingly, for no one enjoys being forced to give. Giving should flow from the heart freely, which is possible only if it is not taken for granted or expected.

CHAPTER 17

PAMPEREd PETS OR VICTIMS of HUMAN ABUSE? By-PASSING THE HEART iN THE TREATMENT of ANIMALS

Since every living creature incorporates its own aspect of divinity in different ways according to its species, we need to recognize this fact in our treatment of all living manifestations of God.

Experiments have indicated that even plants respond either in a positive or negative way to outer stimuli, such as music or human emotions, and react perceptibly to expressions of indifference, dislike, appreciation, or love when it is sent to them.

I once observed a series of experiments designed to prove that plants respond in different ways when a person regularly sends love to one set, hate or curses to another set, and gives no special attention to a third. At the time I was quite skeptical regarding the results of such an experiment, never having given any thought to the possibility that plants could visibly respond to their treatment by human beings. However, as I watched the response of the three batches of plants to these different treatments, I was astonished to see the results. Those on which love was lavished (both mentally and verbally) flourished beyond anyone's expectation, while those receiving no special attention beyond the ordinary daily care grew at their normal rate. However, the most dramatic of the three groups were those plants that received curses, dislike, and even hate. They wilted and died despite the usual provision of water and sunlight given to all three sets. As other similar experiments were undertaken, it became apparent to everyone who heard the results that plants do have the ability to react to different stimuli from people in their close proximity. It also became evident that sounds, and in particular, various types of music, stimulated plants to react visibly in specific ways. For instance, loud music, such as rock and roll, caused them to try to escape from the sound by turning away from the direction from which it was proceeding, whereas with melodious music, especially classical music, they tended to lean toward the source of the sound to which they were responding positively.

The Secret Life of Plants, a book written by Tompkins and Bird,[1] described the many different reactions plants have demonstrated observably.

Since it can be assumed that plants react positively to love and appreciation, and in the opposite way to a lack of love or dislike, surely animals, on their higher step on the evolutionary ladder, are able to react even more dramatically to treatment by their human companions. Here again, the effect of the personal, and thus automatically the general, heart by-pass is acutely apparent.

The treatment of animals can reach extremes, from extravagant over-indulgence all the way to the opposite pole of cruelty, torture, and deprivation.

Animals are forced to rely on their owners for their well-being and protection. They, too, carry within them a spark of divinity, but, unlike humans, they are unable to verbalize their needs, nor can they protest when they are treated cruelly, or rejected by those on whom they depend.

Many people, when they are themselves being controlled, will, in turn, exert harsh control over the animals under their care, in a vain effort to feel less helpless. But it has been taught by all the great world teachers that whatever we do to others, human or otherwise, will, at some time rebound on us according to whether our actions were positive or negative in their effect. Therefore, it is obvious that we all need to be careful how we treat members of primitive species, or we may ourselves receive similar experiences at some time, either in this life or a future one, until we have learned to treat animals with respect and love.

---

[1] Peter Thompkins and Christopher Bird, *The Secret Life of Plants* (New York: HarperCollins, 1989).

Sai Baba has been known to chide a devotee for the harsh treatment of an animal by pointing out that he, too, received the blow or the angry words delivered to the animal, since he and also we are one with all living creatures. He has also said that if we call on the God-self in an animal, it will respond from that aspect and will not harm us. He gives as an example, this delightful story:

> There was once a *guru* who told his disciple that God was in everything. The disciple believed the statement. That very day there was a royal parade. The king was the center of attraction, riding on an enormous elephant. Ignoring the rules of safety for such parades, the disciple planted himself firmly in the path of the royal elephant, and paid no attention to the cries of warning that he would be trampled to death. Upon reaching him, the elephant lifted him and put him safely to one side. The disciple went to his *guru* and complained that although God was in both the elephant and himself, he had been unable to remove the elephant from his path and that, on the contrary, the elephant had removed him. The *guru* explained that it was merely a matter of the elephant having greater physical strength. He told the disciple that, had he not been looking at God in the elephant, the beast would have killed him just as a matter of ordinary work. However, since the disciple was looking at God in the elephant, God had lifted him safely out of harm's way. No animal, not even a cobra, will harm the person who sees God as the essential reality of the animal or the snake. The same is usually true regarding dangerous men, but there are some exceptions here because of *karmic* implications.

But Baba sadly comments that when we call on the God-self in a human being who is about to attack us, the above method is not always as successful, for at this present time no one is totally good; we all are a mixture of good and bad qualities.

Native Americans, Eskimos, and people of similar cultures who still live in close harmony with nature, make it a habit to ask permission of an animal they need to kill for food. There are also many stories about animals who seem to offer their lives to feed starving people. However, the actual killing of an animal is accompanied with specific rituals and prayers, together with thanks to the animal for supplying the much-needed food for survival.

As with children, animals are under our care and protection and should be treated in a caring way. We need to guide and teach them, but should not allow them to control us. We have a responsibility to treat them with consideration for their needs as well as our own.

CHAPTER 18

THE ROLE OF WOMEN IN RE-CONNECTING THE HEART ENERGY

How do we *re-connect* the heart energy that has been cut off or suppressed for centuries in both men and women in all cultures? Women receive the male sperm and bring forth children to replenish the population. They carry the Yin energy, which is receptive, nurturing, and caring in nature. This essentially receptive form also gives them a closer connection to the heart, and to feeling and emotion as distinct from the thinking function.

At this present period in the evolutionary path of the human being, the Yang energy has, of necessity, been over-emphasized and over-developed, often with strong force. But it has now gone too far and needs to be balanced by its opposite but also complementary Yin energy.

This action can be likened to the movement of a pendulum that swings to the limit in one direction and then must swing back just as far in the opposite direction. When this action is allowed to proceed uninterrupted by any block or limitation it will eventually find the center between the two opposites.

At the world level, as well as at the individual human level, this process is always taking place between the opposite pairs of Yin and Yang activity. At the world level, this oscillation is more extreme and therefore involves a longer time span and so is more easily observable.

The most clear-cut example of such wide swings can be seen in the recorded history of nations. Each civilization rises to a peak in all areas of progress only to reverse the direction and gradually collapse. This is a natural process, best exemplified by the life span of all living species, whether crystals, plants, fish, birds, animals, or human beings. The movement of the ocean also follows this rhythm with the Yin ebb or retreat, and the Yang flow or thrust forward.

A very specific timing is involved in this natural ebb and flow in the lives of all creatures. The young are born into this process, live under its action day by day until a peak is reached, when the opposite action starts to take over as they move toward death.

> There is a tide in the affairs of men, which taken at the flood leads on to fortune. Omitted, all the voyage of their life is bound in shallows and in miseries.[1]

We all retain a limited free will that can interfere with this natural rhythm. By being in too much of a hurry, we initiate a counteraction which results in conflict with it. Most of us tend to be in too much of a hurry and try to force the timing to suit our own impatience, and this interferes with the natural flow of the rhythm.

One time when I was in a reverie state, the world beat (or rhythm) was shown to me together with the information that all living things are in sync with it except humans. They, alone, are able with their free will to live separate or apart from its action. This choice is the cause of much of the widespread lack of harmony in the lives of individuals and therefore in world affairs.

So with our free will we have chosen to follow the dictates of the ego and have separated ourselves from this world rhythm. We have identified with our physical and mental bodies, and closed off contact with the world heartbeat, which can connect us to our true identity which is one with It. We need to choose to return, to be in contact with it so that the love that is its identity and power may activate our hearts. This decision can be more easily initiated by women because of a natural ability to incorporate Yin (or receptivity) as their fore-

---

[1] Julius Caesar, lv iii 217.

most aspect, with the Yang (or more active) pole carried within as a support.

As the world pendulum has swung to the Yang pole, it is now essential to remove any obstacles that could prevent its smooth swing back toward the center where all opposites come together into a whole. At such time, it is possible for those who have detached from their dependence on the tangible world to move in consciousness beyond the swing of the pendulum between the two extremes and to be free from the pull of either pole.

This choice would bring to those who wish it, the experience of being united each with their opposite aspect in an inner marriage. The child of that union would have the newborn ability to be free from the control of the pendulum and under the direct influence of the world heartbeat.

Only when more women attain such a balance can they express the love which is the essential essence of the universe. When they begin to allow it to flow through them, they can then direct it to others. The effect will be to re-connect those who are ready to the world heartbeat. This connection will automatically open up other people's hearts to receive this universal force which we call love for lack of a more appropriate and less controversial word.

This opening up of the heart will remove the blocks that prevent love from being received and then shared with others. This reversal will necessarily start slowly, but gain momentum as more people are involved, until it moves faster to change the course of life as we know it. It will bring about a very different kind of revolution than has so far been experienced, and will usher in the new age that prophets and world teachers have called the Golden Age. It will be as if many seeds are planted in Mother Earth and energized by Fathers Sun.

What can women do to help to re-open the heart? First, each one needs to *re-connect* to her own heart and mend the rift that has been in effect for so many centuries.

"Everyone is created equal" is correct, but it is true only at the Hi C level, not at the level of the personality, ego, or body or as a male or female. We have each created the present shell (or container) in which the eternal Self (or flame) is housed. We all have to accept whatever we have assembled into our present personality and learn from it. As we learn, it can be allowed to dissolve to reveal the light that has been hidden within and waiting to be expressed.

For those souls lodged in a female form, the heart (or Yin) expression is their natural path toward wholeness and freedom.

Both men and women can let the Hi C use all four functions, two Yang and two Yin. These functions need to be brought into balance, and this is done when each of them is developed to the fullest possible extent.

How can women initiate this process of opening up their own hearts and then helping others to do the same? There are certain clear and simple activities, which are also used in counselling, that can start to bring about such an opening and *reconnection*.

Listening with the loving ear will start the process, and will encourage more successful communication. Talking is Yang, outgoing activity, while listening is Yin, or receptive.

For as I have mentioned before, most of the people with whom I have worked, whether children, and young adults, those in their middle years, or the aged, complain that no one ever listens when they try to communicate. I have found that listening is perhaps the most helpful part of the process of my work with people. I recall one young man who was about 15 when he came to see me. He had many unresolved questions. He had resisted coming to talk to me at first because, as he expressed it later, he did not want another lecture, as he had his fill of those from both of his parents. I quickly assured him that it was not my intention to give him a lecture, which he found hard to believe and asked, "Then why am I here?" I suggested that he might like to express his problems and any questions he had concerning them and his life. I also assured him that whatever he chose to say would go no further than the room in which we were sitting unless he specifically gave me permission to share any part with his parents or with any other concerned person. I added that I was not there to judge, criticize, or even try to tell him what to do. He was still skeptical as his experience had been the exact opposite. So, I asked, "Would you like to try me?" at which he laughed and accepted that as a fair bargain.

He then proceeded to pour out, in a nonstop stream, everything he had been keeping locked up inside for so long. I made no comments and remained quietly nonjudgmental but supportive. When he finally ran out of words, and with a big sigh relaxed back in his chair, his face lit up with instant comprehension. After a few moments while he was busy processing his insight, he finally said in a soft and hesitant voice, which was in direct contrast to the angry tone with which he began his tirade, "Gosh! I've answered all my own questions, haven't I? You just allowed me to talk. I knew the answers all the time."

The above situation is true of many people, but particularly the youth who all tell me the same thing: that no one really listens to them or gives them their full and undivided attention.

The next step to follow the *loving ear* is to observe how best to offer observations that could be helpful. What *hooks* has a person revealed on which a rope of connection can be thrown? There is not always a single answer to that question. It is important to be patient, until another way is forthcoming to express a suggestion, or present the information until it *clicks*. Otherwise it is useless to proceed to the next point, as each step is like a stepping stone. None of them can be omitted, for there is a learning process connected to each step toward any goal. Shortcuts are not successful in the long run, and are therefore a waste of time and energy. When it is clear that a specific point has been accepted and understood, it is extremely important to make sure that each person understands that they both have the ability to find answers, not just the one offering the *loving ear*. Each one of us has the answers within to solve our own problems, so only by appealing for help from the Hi C can we elicit from It the help we need. Before we can do that, we first have to consider all aspects of the situation under scrutiny with all the methods we have at our disposal. Only when we come to the realization that in spite of doing everything possible to solve it with the help of the conscious mind, we have failed, will we be willing to give up and say with genuine belief that we do not know the answer. Then we will be ready to defer to the Hi C, for we will have removed the ego-based ideas and be able to open up to the superior wisdom of the Hi C.

The role of the person acting as facilitator is to gradually wean the other person away from continued reliance on him or her so that the individual can turn within for the wisdom that is always available. The facilitator tries to create an equal partnership, with each one appealing to the Hi C for help. It is not a matter of telling the person with the problem how to solve it. It should be more along the lines of, "I don't know the answer either, so let us turn together and consult the higher authority."

To my great surprise I have discovered that the many difficulties I have encountered in my life are now proving to be a tremendous asset. People can always sense when someone is speaking from personal experience and not merely from theory. Only when they are sure that the other person not only understands from hearing about the problem, but has encountered a similar problem in the past and has obviously come through it successfully, will there be the necessary trust to proceed. All communication should be a partnership with each partner sharing ideas so that together they can find the answers.

It is necessary that communication be based on *we* and not on *you* or *me*. Only in this way can the barriers be removed that have built up between people, causing them to feel isolated from one another and closed into their individual cells, as if in a prison. All are created equal at the Hi C level. It is only at the outer personality level that people present different behavior patterns, attitudes, and habits.

It is therefore ridiculous for anyone to assume a superior position. Each of us has different functions, activities, and creativity to share. None is more valuable and none is less worthwhile. From this basis, success in communication can take place, but if either one or another feels superior or inferior to the other, free-flowing communication is impossible and the whole attempt is doomed before it is started.

We have all had very different experiences, all of which have given us an opportunity to learn something. What we have learned may possibly be of help to someone else and give them hope of success if they are willing to accept it. They can then be shown that it is possible to find a solution and leave problems behind to proceed to other tasks, which can remove the blocks to creativity and action from which so many people suffer.

We all tend to avoid facing what we consider to be difficult problems. We may suppress them, in which case they drop down into the subconscious, safely out of reach of our conscious attention. Or we conveniently forget them. Another method is to try to soften or deaden the pain the unsolved problems cause, just as we try to alleviate physical pain with an aspirin. In this way, many addictions are started that end up having more serious effects than the original problem.

Avoidance builds tension and requires energy to keep the original problems out of sight. It is obvious that it is preferable to face problems as soon as they arise. We may need to enlist the help of a loving ear to give the necessary temporary support, energy, and encouragement that will enable us to see that whatever is being presented is an opportunity to learn. After the learning, we will be free to proceed to the next step.

It is never too late to go back to the unsolved problems that have created a block to further growth and plunged a person into various avoidance tactics.

Chapter 19

Safe Nest or Steel Trap?

The so-called *nesting* instinct in the females of all species insures that the young are provided with the security they need while they are too young to withstand the problems they will eventually encounter out in the world. Prospective mothers of different species prepare for their young in ways appropriate to their eventual needs.

I remember as a child watching a hen sit on her nest in anticipation of hatching the eggs she would soon lay. Female cats and dogs can also be observed preparing a soft and comfortable place into which to deliver their litter.

Human mothers are known for the frenzied activity in which they are often engaged before the birth of a baby. Many young mothers feel the urge to clean the entire house in preparation for labor. It has become a standard joke that they may even move to a new house shortly before going into labor, so strong is the instinct to prepare a secure home for their helpless baby. Such material needs are, of course, important, but even more so is preparation on a more subtle level to provide a warm welcome for the newcomer about to enter the family scene.

All of the above preparations contribute to a child's feeling of security which is essential for satisfactory development to be achieved. However, if the comforting nest is continued for too long, it becomes like a steel trap and restricts normal growth instead of enhancing it. This unhealthy situation can be observed in families. It can also be observed in many groups that start out with humanitarian objectives, but gradually slip into tight control over the members, which prevents their progress.

The young of all species are taught, by the example of their parents, the various practices that have proved successful in insuring the survival of the species. However, as soon as the young ones are old enough to prove themselves by relying on the early training they received from the parents, and are ready to be on their own and away from the parental supervision, they are pushed out of the nest, lair, or cave to fend for themselves. In this way they gain self-confidence by learning from actual experience that they are capable of surviving on their own. This method is absolutely essential as preparation for full maturity if self-reliance is to be achieved.

All species are instinctively aware of the natural sequence of steps that are necessary for the development from helpless infant to mature adult. If any step is omitted, interrupted, or delayed too long, the individual will not be able to develop normally and will need to continue to rely on the parents for help and direction.

Likewise, human children follow well-defined steps in their growth process. If an illness, accident, or other traumatic event occurs to delay any of these steps, the child will lack the ability that should have been learned at the appropriate time and age.

I am reminded of the work at the Institute for the Development of Human Potential started by Drs. Carl Delacato and Glen Dolman in Philadelphia. This program made use of the natural activities of creeping and crawling in young children, that develop neurological coordination. To spend time creeping and crawling helps those who either didn't do enough of either activity or did them incorrectly during the early years for some reason, such as a birth injury or other trauma. It was noted that if children missed a step in the creeping and crawling sequence they would remain at a stage of development prior to the one that had been omitted. A method was developed whereby children were taught the correct way to creep and crawl to supply the missed steps. With practice, even in older children, the results were most encouraging. For those children who were woefully retarded, usually due to brain damage during the birth process, and could not creep or crawl, a method called patterning was used to supply the missed step. It involved one adult moving each arm and each leg in the appropriate creeping and crawling pattern and one adult moving the head from side to side in rhythm with the arms and legs. Many astonishing examples of complete or partial recovery resulted from the use of this method when a team of caring adults would volunteer to help the parents reprogram a child in need of such treatment.

This program was initiated to help the very obvious cases where a step in the neurological development had been prevented in some unusual way, or from an unforeseen cause, that kept the child from full growth.

However, in many families there is a deliberate intention on the part of one or both parents to keep their children dependent upon them indefinitely for many different reasons.

I have known mothers who prefer their children when they are cute infants and toddlers who need them, so they try to keep them at that stage for their own selfish pleasure. They hate to see them grow up and begin to show a need for independence, and would prefer always to have a baby to care for. So they either try to keep them dependent, or they have more babies so that they always have a little one in the house, whether they can afford it or not. Obviously, this is not an expression of love, but extreme cruelty stemming from selfishness. Children who are kept at an immature level find it very difficult to live in the world, especially after their parents are no longer present to direct them and make their decisions for them. In the name of love such parents have literally crippled the children they profess to love so much. The crippling, unlike the physical kind which can readily be seen and therefore can be handled in some way, is invisible, which makes them even more helpless, since they are expected to perform as if they were normal.

When we are children learning to become responsible citizens, we all need guidelines to steer us in the right direction, for we are born helpless infants needing a secure environment in order to develop normally, but as children grow older they need to be freed from such dependence on others.

If the family situation was such that children are loth to leave it for the often harsh reality of the world outside of its protection, they may endeavor to find replacements in a work or learning environment that will provide a similar sense of security. Or, they may use illness to insure that a safe nest will continue to be provided. Many people use sickness to force others to act as surrogate parents.

Some adult children choose to continue to live at home where care is assured, and they will even delay marrying unless they can find someone who will be wiling to give them a similar secure nest.

These are just a few examples to show the effect of nests that have been too secure for too long. They can cause grown children to be trapped in dependency, and it is difficult to escape from such a situation.

Not only can parents provide safe nests for their young and then continue to keep them nest-bound, but many institutions fall into a similar pattern. They start out by undertaking to protect and give security and help to groups of people who come under their supervision. The original motive and concept may be thoroughly praiseworthy, but unfortunately, the actual outcome frequently develops into a very different situation.

Let us take as an example workers' unions, which were first established to provide protection for workers. These unions were formed to prevent employers from taking advantage of employees by over-working them, or under-paying them, or expecting them to work in unsafe conditions. In the beginning the unions were instrumental in raising the standard of working conditions in many areas. They provided a safe and secure place for those who might otherwise be underprivileged. But, like the family nest, the unions began to gain more and more control, not only over the employers but eventually over the workers whom they had agreed to help. The *carrot* they dangled as bait was a promise of more benefits that were not always forthcoming, in exchange for lack of freedom.

Universities can also fall into a similar category. They set out to provide an education for the students under their care. But to those students who are looking for another safe nest on leaving the one made available by their parents, they become a steel trap in which dependent young people continue to remain long after they should be ready to take all they have learned out into the world to share their knowledge with others. Some become perpetual students, afraid to leave the comparative safety of the learning establishment they have chosen to supply their continued need for a nest.

Religious institutions can exert a similar influence on their members. Religions start out with a wonderfully inspiring message which holds out a promise of security, comfort, help, freedom, and happiness. People flock to the shelter they hope will keep them safe from the harsh world and from their personal problems. But instead of teaching that everyone has within them a source of inspiration, help, and guidance, the elders of various churches may start to take control. They set forth innumerable rules for the parishioners to follow and promise them salvation if they abide by them. Thus again, a secure nest eventually becomes a steel trap in which the unsuspecting are caught like fish in a net, afraid to break free, yet disillusioned by the apparently broken promises of those they had trusted.

In peacetime the various branches of the armed forces present an example of a ready-made nest to some people. Their daily needs are met and there are few decisions they are required to make, for the daily routine is already set for them. They settle into a way of life containing very little uncertainty. The original purpose was to provide security and safety for the whole population, but during relatively peaceful times, like other nests turned into traps, a career in a branch of the military can lock these national protectors in their own steel traps.

Dictatorships present another example. A benevolent parental figure sets out to provide liberally for his people by rescuing them from poverty, malnutrition, and oppression, assuring them of a safe and secure environment with him acting as their caring parent. Of course, the underprivileged will fall for such assurances, hoping to improve their lot and that of their families. What have they got to lose when they are so needy? But, like other promised security blankets, the enticing promises carry as a price tag the loss of their personal freedoms, and for many, it becomes too high a price to pay.

Whenever a governing body or organization inhibits people's freedom to be creative and assume responsibility for themselves, it automatically results in a nest that degenerates into a trap.

The welfare system is another example of help backfiring and creating an intolerable situation for everyone concerned; those who are supposed to benefit, and the general public faced with ever-increasing taxes to pay for it. Like many other institutions, it started out to supply temporary security through financial support to people who are in the unfortunate position of being unable to support themselves and their family. However, when continued indefinitely, welfare robs people of the chance to improve their lot and become independent from such aid so they continue to live at a woefully low level of existence.

To my surprise, I have known people who actually used hospitals and mental institutions as nests rather than face life on their own. Some people would rather be cared for in such establishments than develop their own abilities, and become independent and free from such reliance.

For some people, prisons can also be used as an alternative to independence, and though prisons certainly do not provide a comfortable nest, it is often more secure than the life the inmates had been living before their incarceration.

Even a country's possession of nuclear weapons can provide its population with the illusion of safety from attack by other countries and the dreaded ordeal of a war with all the attendant privations.

Nests that have become steel traps contribute to the personal heart by-pass by keeping those who are caught in them at an immature stage of development. This prevents the heart from being opened to express love to others.

PART II

The Heart By-Pass in Public Institutions

CHAPTER 20

THE HEART BY-PASS IN EDUCATION

So far we have been examining the effect of the heart by-pass in the various relationships in our personal lives and how we as individuals relate to one another. We are also conditioned by many impersonal factors, so we need to see what impact the lack of caring in industries, organizations, establishments, institutions, and corporations, to name but a few, have on our lives. For, like it or not, we all live under their control and cannot escape them or ignore them since institutions of all kinds are a major part of our society, and to a large extent dictate the quality or lack of it in our lives and therefore in the life of our country.

As we look around, it is all too evident that there is very little love in action in these conglomerates. The stupendous task of attempting to bring about changes in such giants is disheartening, to put it mildly. If we look at the whole unwieldy problem, trying to make the much-needed changes will seem to be an impossible undertaking to attempt alone. However, if just one individual in each massive group could *re-connect* his or her own heart, and bring more consideration and genuine caring into his or her small area of activity, it could act like the small amount of yeast that is capable of raising a large mass of dough when we make bread.

First of all, we need to examine our own lives to determine if we are contributing to the heart by-pass in our relationships. If so, we do not have to wait until we are perfect and no longer guilty of closing our hearts before we get involved. We need only start this *re-connecting* process, and it will be sensed by many people we meet, whether they are consciously aware of it or not. When unselfish love is shown to people, they start to open up like flowers to sunshine, for most people are starving for this kind of nourishment.

The changes may be painfully slow, for lifelong habits are not readily relinquished. But eventually it will be like the proverbial snowball that starts out very small, and gains momentum as it rolls along and gathers around it more and more snow. This small beginning will expand and reach more people who have been unknowingly waiting for a chance to improve the quality of their lives—to have more loving and meaningful relationships with others.

Many such small beginnings can form a network that can expand to reach all parts of the world. People who participate may not necessarily know one another, but each one can act like a small lamp to bring light into the surrounding darkness. So let us look at the many areas where such an action needs to take place.

First, it is essential to evaluate the educational systems throughout the world. They are the breeding grounds that determine how children will develop. The young people of every nation who will be entering the various institutions in their countries are the ones who could initiate the necessary changes, but only if they are properly prepared for such a task. At present, students who are the products of the education provided by the schools and colleges the world over are being taught to perpetuate the heart by-pass by concentrating exclusively on intellectual pursuits and neglecting their hearts. This system creates an imbalance between the Yin and Yang in each of them and therefore in the world around them. In order to facilitate the necessary changes, students everywhere must be given a more balanced regime so that they can prepare for future changes. As Baba says, "Education is not for a mere living, but for a fuller and meaningful life."

At present, even very young children in kindergarten are already imbued with the concept of competitiveness. Many parents start this conditioning shortly after their children are born. Young parents watch the babies of their friends and acquaintances to see if their own children are equally advanced, even in the very early steps in development that naturally vary with each individual child. The parents often take it person-ally when their child does not take the first step or say the first word at the same age as someone else's child. Children are quick to sense this fierce competitiveness in their parents and react in different ways to such pressure to succeed. Some strain to please their parents by becoming overachievers, oth-ers rebel and refuse to compete, and still others feel inadequate and stop trying rather than dealing with the possibility of be-ing unsuccessful.

These early patterns continue into adulthood unless at some point they are recognized and faced, and a decision is made to move beyond their inhibiting influence. The educa-tion system, as it stands, exacerbates the problem and imprints competitiveness even more deeply on students who have al-ready been programmed by ambitious, competitive parents.

This kind of control originates from selfishness and a lack of true concern for the children's welfare. Parents must realize that what is appropriate for each child is more important than what enhances their own self-esteem. It takes very brave par-ents to flout such rigid conditioning, but as more parents be-come concerned for their children's well-being, and not just their scholastic achievements, they will break away from this traditional approach. When this concept is accepted by more parents, they will achieve a strong enough force to demand that the education system change to benefit the children.

From such a small beginning great changes can be wrought, for like the hundredth monkey, it takes only that first one to start the ball rolling. As schools and colleges change the current system in which mental achievement is stressed and the heart is ignored, many more young people will be pre-pared to raise the level of consciousness by *re-connecting* their hearts.

Sai Baba has already initiated such a process in India. At his ashram in Andhra Pradesh, he has started schools from kindergarten up to the college level. They are based on his human values program, which is taught in addition to the usual academic subjects. The students who have been trained under Baba's revolutionary system go forth into society well-equipped to bring about the necessary changes wherever they are even-tually employed. They will be able to accomplish such changes by their own example, as others observe the way they live when they incorporate the five main values in Baba's program into everything they do. By striving to be honest, acting in a way that is correct for each situation, letting love flow from within into their surroundings and to all those with whom they come in contact, behaving peacefully whatever the provocation to react negatively, and avoiding any kind of violence (whether mental, emotional, verbal, or physical), they will be examples to others.

In contrast, most students go into future jobs or occupations heavily programmed, first by their early upbringing by parents and other family members, followed by the education they receive in the schools and colleges they attend. The present system obviously has not succeeded in producing well-rounded students, for it turns out men and women who are discontented, unfulfilled, and without a sense of direction in their lives. The one-sided, limited, and machine-like way of life we see around us is not making people happy, nor is it helping the state of the world.

Restructuring the education system is the first step in correcting this situation, since the education system is the basis for all other systems in our society. As we change our values and open up our hearts we can change the world by giving people hope and encouraging them to become more humane.

CHAPTER 21

THE ABSENCE OF HEART IN GOVERNMENT

Education is only one of the many areas over which government has control and for which specific funds need to be allocated. Obviously the priorities of all the members of the governing body will influence the final apportioning of available funds for any given program. But as the various members are themselves all products of the present system of education, they have been exposed to the by-pass of the heart and the concentration on intellectual pursuits. They have been trained to make decisions with the intellect, with little input from the heart. Policies are decided almost exclusively by the rational mind, instead of including and considering what is best for their constituents.

There are many other factors that also color governmental decisions. For example, the men and women who comprise the different sections of the government are, just like everyone else, prone to self-interest and self-service. So, if certain decisions they are considering could result in the loss of their position and the salary they receive from it, they will hesitate to act.

It is interesting to note that whenever the question is raised concerning the desirability of many of the programs that directly affect our lives, the same answer is invariably forthcoming, namely, "We give the people what they ask for." It has become a vicious circle, and until more people begin to exert their rights to question the many and varied controls under which they live, the situation cannot be improved.

Those of us who do care about our present and future welfare, and the welfare of our families, and the people in the rest of the world, are being given an opportunity to make a stand against the accelerating encroachment of control, as if by a giant brain or computer, with no care for the quality of life for the individuals who comprise each community or country.

It is a sheer waste of time to blame the government for the problems that beset us. We are all indirectly responsible for them, so we are the ones who must address them and endeavor to help solve them by being willing to be heard. No changes will occur, as if by magic, unless we unite to demand them. Baba says, "Either the government must have the capacity to educate and reform the people, or the people must have the capacity to educate the government."

It is not the purpose of this book to attempt to include all the ways our lives are being controlled by the thinking and planning of those in positions of authority. Yes, the heart energy is absent wherever we look. But those of us who understand the acute seriousness the effect this lack of love is having on people are the very ones who can start to bring about small changes which will lead to the major ones so desperately needed in every area of our lives.

We are not helpless or insignificant, for our true identity is measureless whenever we call upon It to manifest in our thoughts, feelings, words and deeds every day of our lives. Wherever we live or work, we **can** make a difference, so it is up to each of us to accept this fact and act accordingly as we are directed from within when we seek guidance from our Self.

CHAPTER 22

THE HEART BY-PASS IN FINANCE

What role does money play in relation to the heart by-pass? When Sai Baba called me for an interview specifically to outline his Ceiling on Desires Program, he clarified the role of money, which has been misunderstood by many people.

He told me that money, of itself, is not the root of all evil, as the old saying would have us believe. He explained that money is a form of energy, and like any other energy, it is neutral—neither good nor bad. Just as electricity, for example, can be utilized to heat a house, cook a meal, or light a room, all uses we would agree are positive ones, it can also be used to injure, and even kill.

Likewise, Baba said that food is a form of energy, but it, too, can either nourish the person who partakes of it, or conversely, it can cause illness or even death if it is contaminated or stale.

If money is energy and therefore neutral, why, throughout the ages, has it been dubbed the source of all evil? Money is not evil; the way it is used by those who have responsibility for it may be evil. It can produce either a positive or a negative result, according to the intent of those who use it. So it is not money, but those who are in charge of its use who make it beneficial or evil in its effect. In the right hands it can be a great blessing, whereas in the wrong hands it can become a veritable curse. So we need to see how it can be used for evil purposes and how it can be utilized to benefit both the user and those who are affected by it.

Baba teaches that money should not be wasted, but used in service to humanity to improve our living conditions. Many people use money to accumulate more attachments, acquiring more and more possessions in the hope of finding security. Such acquisitiveness is tantamount to an attempt to carry an extremely heavy piece of luggage all day long every day throughout an entire life without a moment's freedom from the weighty load. Such a habit is guaranteed to lead eventually to bitter disappointment and a feeling of emptiness, for tangible possessions cannot satisfy their owner permanently since their very nature is impermanent.

As with all other forms of energy, money is being wasted or used inappropriately in every aspect of life, and in all parts of the world. If such widespread waste could be halted, people all over the world would benefit. However, we cannot afford to be critical of other people, or the government, if we are also guilty of wasting money in our private lives.

Baba has provided the Ceiling on Desires Program, brilliantly designed to help everyone who is willing to use it, to contribute their share to the removal of waste in the four categories of money, food, time, and energy. By starting to practice his program, we can begin to make a difference, for our personal contribution, when multiplied by many thousands of other people's efforts, must have a strong impact.

For those who jump to the erroneous conclusion that Baba advocates our being reduced to abject poverty by following such a program, nothing could be further from the truth. Far too many people have been taught that poverty goes hand in hand with spirituality, and that it is not "spiritual" to have money and possessions. Actually, to choose poverty in the mistaken belief that it is a more "spiritual" way to live, while expecting other people to supply our needs, can be a block to spiritual progress. Having money or lacking it is not the problem. It can be an obstacle on our inner path if we become attached to it as our security, or allow it to dominate us. When we are free from its control over us, we can use money in many different helpful ways. Then it becomes a blessing rather than a hindrance on our path.

Baba stresses the necessity for "Seva," or service, which means that everything we do should have service as the motive instead of the sum of money we will receive for our labors. The present pervading custom of doing as little as possible and expecting to earn as much as possible needs to be reversed. When an increasing number of people look upon their work as a form of worship by dedicating it to their inner Hi C and allowing It to act through them, the overall handling of money will begin to improve. Then there can be sufficient funds to serve the people, whether through a financial budget reserved for education, or in other ways.

So let us stop the useless habit of blaming other people, fate, or the government for the ills that we see around us. We can start to put our own lives in order.

We all tend to carry our possessions around with us. We also treat the people in our lives as if we owned them. We need to remember that they are only borrowed for our use in this present lifetime. So, as Baba says, we must be willing to jettison possessions and attachments along with all the overlay that we carry on our shoulders, for it obscures our light from view, and keeps us from lighting our way back to union with our source.

It appears to be easier when we have no possessions, but having them, and remaining detached from their control, is actually more beneficial toward our growth.

Vanished—Long Lost Luggage

Interestingly enough, I had a personal experience of actually being without luggage on a recent visit to Germany. I had planned to be there for a month to give seminars on my work and a number of talks at various Sai Centers.

At the start of the trip I checked my suitcases at the Los Angeles airport, watched as they went on their way on the moving belt and received the usual luggage tags to enable me to retrieve them when I landed at my destination. However, upon arriving at the Frankfurt airport, the large suitcase containing my clothes for the next month, as well as some of the articles I use in the seminars, did not arrive off the luggage ramp. With the help of the friend who met me, we reported the missing piece and several inquiries were made by the airport personnel, but the bag was not found. I was assured that the loss would be reported over the worldwide computer system, and that when the bag was located, it would be sent on to me wherever I was at the time.

I realized with a shock that I would have to proceed on my journey without it. I had only the clothes in which I had traveled and one change of clothing in my overnight bag. How was I to manage to give seminars and talks for a month in the very cold weather at that time of the year in Germany where there was snow in many of the areas where I would be visiting? What a dilemma!

However, I quickly realized that I was free to choose how I would react, as I have learned that we are all free to decide what attitude to assume and how we meet the experiences we face. Here I was with a seemingly insoluble problem, so how was I going to choose to react to it? I could lose my temper and rage at the airline for losing my luggage, but what good would that do? It would only make me very nervous and upset, but it would not bring back my case. Or I could dissolve into tears of self-pity over how unfair it was to have such a loss occur when I was willing to travel long distances by plane to other countries to share the work I had been taught. I could also ask,"Why me?" and become depressed at the turn that fate had taken. But that attitude would not bring a solution either. In my work I have been taught to stop indulging in the common habit of blaming other people, fate, or conditions in the outer world for situations and experiences, and, instead, ask what could be learned from each incident and what attitude would be appropriate under any given circumstance. I have shared this practice with others, so now I knew I must use the same advice myself.

I turned my attention away from the crisis and asked within for help. In this way I lifted the burden from my shoulders and surrendered it to the Hi C or Baba within, who knew exactly why it had happened, what it was to teach me, and how to proceed. So I mentally said, "I have arrived in Germany to give seminars on my work and talks at Sai gatherings for a month. My luggage containing all my warm clothes is missing. I have done all I can to locate it, but to no avail. Please help." With that, I literally let go of the problem and thus relieved, I was able to proceed light-heartedly and consider the whole episode as a joke.

I did try to buy some replacement clothes, but was greeted at each store with the news that all the warm clothes had been sold a month ago in the January sales, and only summer weight clothes were available. This was no help to me in the cold weather, particularly in places where there was snow.

Then, the most amazing thing started to happen. Various women, some of whom I already knew, but others who heard of my situation, either gave or lent me clothes to wear during the visit, so I was supplied with what I needed by their kindness. Even a photograph of Baba was presented to me with the remark that my own photographs were probably also in my lost luggage, which was correct.

This entire incident proved beyond a shadow of a doubt that we will be provided with what we need if we are willing to ask within for help. Many people told me that the lesson was valuable for them, too.

Whether it is a so-called possession we have lost, or a person we love, they are all in our present life only temporarily and for our mutual learning. So we need to hold them lightly, and be ready to let go whenever the time arrives for them to be taken from us. For, as Baba says, "Freedom is independence from externals. One who is in need of the help of another person, thing or condition is a slave thereof. Perfect freedom is not given to any man on earth, because the very meaning of mortal life is relationship with and dependence on another. The lesser the number of wants, the greater the freedom. Hence, perfect freedom is absolute desirelessness."

This does not mean we should eliminate relationships and possessions, as that seemingly easy way out would merely be an escape from learning what only they can teach us. We cannot live in a vacuum. We need people and objects as our teachers and our tests. As Baba says, it is *dependence* on them that prevents us from being free.

Since the loss of my luggage I have been dealing with the insurance company that is handling the claim. So, I have been learning from firsthand experience how the heart by-pass operates in insurance companies.

In my case, I try to live as closely as possible to the teachings of Baba and of my reverie work in all phases of my life. I tried to be meticulous in filling out the numerous forms that were requested, supplying as many of the receipts for purchases as were still available, and checking with various stores to ascertain the probable replacement costs of all the lost articles. I naively assumed that because I had been paying my premiums regularly for many years, and had not been obliged to report any major loss prior to this one, that there would be no problem with my claim being accepted.

How wrong I was! In spite of the care and honesty with which I completed the report, it was questioned. I was asked to produce even more proof that I had purchased all the listed articles of clothing. After completing still more lists, I was informed that I needed to send photographs of myself wearing the various pieces of clothing, as well as affidavits from people who could vouch for the fact that they had seen me wearing them. At that point I decided to take a firm stand on my rights as someone who had paid the premiums regularly and who was not trying to cheat the company.

Baba tells us that if we overlook a wrong and do nothing to point it out or correct it we are as responsible for it as the one who is at fault. So I asked the insurance representative to explain the situation. I was informed that the stringent requirements were based on the fact that some people who had suffered a similar loss had not been honest in their reports. These people padded their list of lost clothing to include expensive items that were not contained in their lost luggage. The dishonesty of a few unscrupulous people has now created problems for others who report their losses accurately.

This unfortunate situation shows how people with closed hearts can affect entire companies, creating corporate policies which also by-pass the heart.

Once again, we can only look at our own lives to be sure we are acting from our hearts. Those of us in policy-making positions must try to keep our hearts open in each decision we make and not just operate out of the head, rigidly closing out people who need our help because a few dishonest ones have created problems in the past. The rest of us must realize the effects of our actions and resolve not to take advantage of others, either large impersonal insurance companies or those closer to home.

Chapter 24

The "Live Happily Ever After" Myth

One time in a reverie, I was shown the immense thought form built around the myth that when we meet the right person we will live happily ever after. The first thing I learned was that fairy tales and myths relate to a quest for an inner partner, and not the outer one of searching for another person to fulfill our needs. We have to seek within to discover the other part of ourselves. We need to connect with this inner part to enable us to become whole. In an inner marriage, the separate parts will eventually merge so that we can then allow the Hi C to use us as a whole person for Its instrument.

All the romantic myths and fairy tales, such as the knight in shining armor, Cinderella, Sleeping Beauty, and the eternal quest for the lover and the loved one, are very confusing if taken literally. These myths are the indirect cause of unrequited love, various insecurities, a feeling of not rating, or of something being wrong or missing if no outer partner is available, all of which undermines a person's confidence. The belief that another person will be like a magic wand to bring about the solution to every problem is a falsehood, and we have all been programmed with this myth. The fantasy that life would be perfect with this other person causes us to try to live in the future instead of attending to each day as it comes, and watching for the signs and opportunities to show us the next steps in our journey.

This "Live Happily Ever After" myth was shown to me in the reverie as a thought form. It appeared to be completely unsubstantial, like soap bubbles blown from a child's toy pipe, or like a scene made from tissue paper, froth, or cotton candy. When I attempted to mentally enter this scene, I found there was nothing solid to it. Everything about this myth lets people down and disappoints them.

Then I was shown the opposite side to this myth. I saw what happens when it is proved to be unreliable. I also had to enter the thought form around this part to determine how it felt. I descended into a sticky layer that reminded me of the Los Angeles smog, dark brown and dense, and composed of all the dreams and illusions that had gone awry. Disillusionment appeared as a sticky toxic state.

These were the two sides to the thought form I experienced. When the myth disappoints because someone cannot find that perfect partner, or cannot change the current partner to be the way he or she wants, the person often turns against any kind of partnership and is angry at fate for the disappointment.

I realized that most people are caught as if in a net or a cobweb in the "perfect partner" fantasy. But it is also like a morass composed of disappointment when it does not support their dream of happiness. It is like being on a see-saw or a pendulum that swings from one extreme to the other.

Only when we are able to be centered directly in the middle between these two opposites can we take the inner journey of the soul in search of its other half and be at peace. This was the truth being presented in the fairy tales and myths, but they have been taken literally, and this has caused untold sorrow to so many hopeful people. Only when we are released from the thrall of this thought form will we be able to open up our hearts without the fear of being hurt. When we seek within for our inner partner, only happiness can be the result, as there is nothing and no one to cause hurt or rejection.

I was also shown that this does not mean we cannot have an outer partner, but that he or she should be one who will help us along our own path, and we should be willing to do likewise. Neither partner can change the other into the person they are seeking, for it is not the outer partner, but the inner other half of themselves that they seek. If we understand this, we will not be tempted to try to bend another to our wishes, to use love potions, threats, promises, blackmail, and all the other ploys to force the love of another.

Chapter 25

The Food Industry

It used to be possible to buy food in its natural state—without chemicals and other additives. Farmers and produce gardeners would fertilize their crops with natural substances, and because there was no vast network of international transportation, food was sold and consumed locally. This meant that the preservatives currently so widely used were not necessary. The local people would eat what was available during the productive season. To provide for the winter months, when there was a dearth of fruits and vegetables, people preserved them by drying, pickling, canning, or making them into jams and compotes. Now we are able to buy many foods that are out of season, for they are flown in from other areas of the country or other parts of the world where the climate is conducive to year-round crops, or the seasons are opposite to ours.

To protect foods being shipped all over the world, the food is treated with various chemicals. The addition of preservatives prevents food from spoiling, so it reduces waste and provides many people with needed nourishment who might otherwise starve or suffer from malnutrition. In this respect, the addition of chemicals can be a helpful and considerate practice. On the other hand, many foods are treated with chemicals in addition to preservatives. Coloring substances make the food item more pleasing to the eye, but it can also have a deleterious effect on the consumers, as can various flavoring agents. Nitrites and nitrates abound. Many insecticides sprayed on crops remain in the soil from one crop to the next. Some farmers plant soybeans in fields which have been saturated with insecticides because soybeans have the ability to absorb certain chemicals and thus remove them from the soil. However, when the soybeans are eaten, these chemicals are also ingested, so unknowingly we are being poisoned by the very food we eat to stay healthy.

Bananas are cut while they are still green. To prevent them from ripening too fast and spoiling before they are delivered to the markets, they are sprayed with a chemical solution to delay ripening. But then they are sprayed again with another chemical solution upon arrival at their destination to accelerate the ripening process. Thus, people who eat bannanas are exposed to various chemicals without their knowledge. Many people experience allergic reactions and have no idea of the possible cause of their symptoms, so they have no way of avoiding a future attack.

Other kinds of fruit and vegetables, particularly apples, are sprayed with arsenic and other insecticides to repel insect pests that might destroy them. We eat the arsenic and other poisons with the apples and other foods.

Another problem, especially for people who suffer from allergies, is the addition of many substances to cans, packaged foods, frozen foods, fast foods, as well as food served in many restaurants. MSG (Monosodium glutamate) is one additive to which many people react adversely. They experience headaches, nausea, and confused thinking. MSG used to be primarily used in Chinese restaurants and was first called the Chinese Restaurant Syndrome. It is a taste enhancer, so it gives more flavor to foods. It is sold in many markets and from time to time has been banned by the FDA as hazardous to health. However, its use has gradually crept back because many people want their food to be tasty, and not everyone reacts to MSG with allergic symptoms.

So, besides the reactions of known allergy sufferers to some substances, many other people are at risk when they eat foods or drink beverages treated with additives that are injurious to health.

We cannot change the practices of the entire food industry, but we can protect our family and ourselves as much as possible by refusing to buy questionable products. It does take time and patience to read every label to check the contents of canned, packaged, and frozen foods, but it is essential to be willing to do so if we want to protect our health. This is another way of expressing love, for it shows that we care enough to take the necessary precautionary measures to insure the family's safety.

It is clear that the original intention was to preserve food and to protect the consumers from diseases caused by unsafe food. However, it would appear the stronger, but more selfish motive of making more money has prevailed in the food industry. Because of this situation, we are all faced with the personal responsibility of being careful when selecting the food we and our families consume. We can avoid processed and preserved foods and eat foods that are in season. In this way we can all work together and avoid foods that contain injurious chemicals and insist that the farmers provide food that is organically grown.

CHAPTER 26

THE HEART BY-PASS IN MEDICINE

One of the most important influences in my life while I was growing up in England was a wonderful man whom I always called Doccie. He was a general practitioner and was married to my mother's oldest sister. I used to spend my school holidays with them, and one of my fondest memories was of accompanying him on his rounds when he visited patients who were too ill to go to his surgery for treatment. They lived in the north of England in a coal mining district, so many of his patients were miners and their families. He was loved by every one of them as he took with him much more than his medical skills with which to treat them. He always had a cheery word for each one and knew all about their lives, children, heartaches, and sorrows, for he cared for the whole person and not just the sick body.

Many of his patients were so poor that they could not afford to pay even his very low fees. So he was often presented with a bag of potatoes that had been grown in the tiny allotments they cultivated in the odd minutes they were able to spare from their long hours down in the coal mines. Or they might shyly hand him a jar of preserved fruit or jam made from the fruit of a tree they had carefully cultivated. I, of course, was fascinated and always curious to see what would be handed to him with a tentative smile, by a donor who was obviously anxious to see if the gift was large enough to compensate him for his ministration, yet not able to offer more, for even these small donations were a drain on their meager rations.

Doccie never refused a call for help. He would see patients in his surgery all day long and then sally forth on his rounds to visit those who could not go to him. For every one of them he had a cheerful smile and words of encouragement. Each patient was a well-known human being to him, and no one was rejected or refused treatment.

These early experiences of observing the way he practiced his profession were, for me, the model of how a doctor should be. Idealistic as I was as a child, I idolized him, and my fondest dream was to become a doctor when I grew up; but that was not to happen.

Nowadays, as I look around me and hear about some of the experiences of others, I am saddened to realize how drastically the medical scene has changed. The practice of medicine has been reduced to a business where the goal often appears to be to make as much money as possible instead of concentrating on helping those who appeal for treatment for some kind of illness. The result of a prime quest for money is for a doctor to see as many patients as can be fitted into a specific time frame at his office. Obviously such a schedule does not allow adequate time for the doctor to get to know the patient or observe the life-style, habits, or family situation, or how these may be contributing to the person's symptoms. The patient is merely one number in an assembly line of patients. So instead of relying on the diagnostic ability of the doctor, each patient is given innumerable tests designed to try to ascertain the cause of his malaise. Machines determine the ailment and replace the personal touch of a caring human being.

In addition to this dehumanization of the medical profession, the ever-increasing arsenal of drugs replaces the natural remedies that were formerly in use and which, besides usually alleviating the suffering, did not cause extra problems as so many of the drugs can do with their frequent side effects.

The situation currently seen in hospitals is another glaring example of the lack of heart in the field of medicine or healing. Patients are often treated in an impersonal way as if they were inanimate objects, devoid of nerves or feelings.

It is a frightening prospect to face being admitted to a hospital in the first place, but once installed as a number in a bed in a room, it can be even more intimidating to a person who is already suffering from a serious illness. The patient has left the security of home and family, is all alone among strangers, and is about to undergo innumerable tests to determine the cause of the present illness, all at a cost that the patient may not be able to afford.

I am reminded of the hospital built to Sai Baba's instructions at his ashram in India, which is one of the most primitive countries in respect to hygiene. But at that hospital the patient is not left all alone upon admittance. It is the custom for members of the family to stay with patients to take care of their needs when these are not being provided by the busy hospital staff. Family members are present when their relative goes to be given the prescribed tests and they are waiting for the patient's return. No one is left alone to deal with very natural fears associated with being in a hospital.

On the other side of the coin, many Western doctors report that they have been forced to rely more and more on standard tests due to the huge increase in the amount of insurance they have to assume because of the incidence of lawsuits initiated by patients on the slightest excuse for imagined as well as actual malpractice. Here, again, the lack of heart is in evidence when patients rush to bring a lawsuit against a doctor as an opportunity to obtain a large settlement. This practice creates problems for the people who have legitimate claims and who are sometimes refused the costs of medical expenses because of other patients' dishonesty.

False insurance claims, and some insurance companies' overconcern with retaining as much profit as possible, contribute to the lack of care for those in need of financial help to which they are entitled, especially when they have paid their insurance premiums. In both of these instances the heart has been closed off, leaving only the brain active in making decisions.

Instead of blaming others, each of us can examine our own motives. Are we guilty of dishonesty? We are only able to change our own questionable practices. We cannot directly change those of other people or companies, but we do have a responsibility to point out wrong-doing when it is brought to our attention. Singly, we may feel helpless to make changes, but when many people join in a united effort to correct errors, the force of their numbers has more power to bring about the necessary improvements in policy.

CHAPTER 27

HEART BY-PASS IN RELIGIONS

All of the main religions have a principal message that everyone should do to others only what they themselves would want others to do to them. Yet, as we look around the world, we cannot help but wonder what has happened to this universal message. We see the exact opposite in operation everywhere. Just as individuals concentrate mainly on what is good for them personally, the same selfish attitude can be observed between countries and their leaders in their dealings with one another.

If we are all one at the Source, whatever we do to someone else we are actually doing to ourselves, whether on a personal or a national level. This rule is outlined by the laws of karma which dictate that whatever we put out into the world, whether hurtful or helpful, will at some time in the future rebound on us and cause us to experience exactly what we originally sent out to others by our thought, word, or deed. So instead of blaming fate or other people for our problems, we really have only ourselves to blame or thank for whatever happens to us.

Religious concepts can be likened to signposts or ground rules, but if we only hear them expounded or read about them in the scriptures and holy books, and do not put these concepts into practice in our personal lives, they cannot help us. Their message is loud and clear. We are the ones who have chosen to close off our hearts and act contrary to the teachings.

However, in most organized religions the clergy or elders are in a power position between the words of the scriptures on the one hand, and the members of the congregation or organization, on the other. They are responsible for explaining the meaning of a particular teaching so that it is fully understood by the majority of the congregation. But they have often been the very people who have distorted the original meaning and even at times suppressed some teachings because they did not agree with them, or they did not want them known.

Again, the subject of control is raised, for people who are given power can very easily be seduced by it. Instead of using a position of authority to help followers on their chosen path, some religious leaders set forth an array of rules to be followed blindly, and seekers may not have the privilege of asking any questions. They may also present the teachings factually, without explaining the original truths which were invariably given in symbolic form.

Groups that form around a religious ideal often omit any reference to the fact, included in so many of the ancient texts, that we are all one at the level of the inner essence (or Hi C) and that eventually everyone who is ready and willing should be left free to defer to their own teacher. Nor do they teach that spiritual seekers should gradually be weaned away from reliance on outer teachers who are often at variance with the One within. Some of the leaders in the churches, temples, synagogues, and other meeting places are not considering the welfare of the individual members of their congregation. They often concentrate only on their position of assumed authority to expound the scriptures. This mental approach causes their hearts to be closed.

Thus the hearts of both the clergy and their parishioners are by-passed. The people are misled about their true identity and prevented from being taught by contact with the love that is available from that inner source.

As with other institutions, individually, we cannot change these practices. But we are all free to decide the values according to which we wish to live. We can also choose to seek within for contact with our Real Self, to allow Its love to open our hearts, and to let that expansive love flow out into our surroundings, to the people in our lives, and to all parts of the world where it is so needed.

When I conduct seminars on my work, I start each session with a group exercise or meditation using the symbol of a Maypole as an aid. All those who wish to participate are asked to imagine they are taking one of the ribbons attached to the top of the maypole. They can choose a ribbon of any color they prefer. The ribbon acts like a telephone connection to the multiple Hi C visualized at the top of the maypole where all the ribbons are attached. I suggest that the participants mentally ask the Hi C to pour down the chosen ribbon Its unconditional love, which can then be directed to any people they know who are ill or unhappy, and to all parts of the world where healing and comfort are lacking. This exercise, which takes only a few minutes to practice, is a service anyone can give. When it is multiplied by the efforts of many people, it will make a difference and will remove the helpless feeling that many of us suffer in the face of worldwide distress.

This can be a simple but very practical form of prayer that can be undertaken individually or in a group.

CHAPTER 28

HEART BY-PASS IN ORGANIZATIONS

Since the heart by-pass is so prevalent, it operates in every aspect of life wherever people are interacting with one another. It is particularly evident in the various organizations that unite many people under one theme.

Since I have chosen to follow Sai Baba's teaching and guidance, I frequently find myself in a group of his devotees, for Baba advocates *sathsang*, which means associating with others of like mind as reminders of the teachings that need to be practiced. However Baba says that he can count his true devotees on the fingers of one hand, they are so rare. The vast majority of those who follow him are in the process of learning to put his teachings into practice in their lives and in their relationships with others, whether casual acquaintances, relatives or friends.

Unfortunately, a misconception has arisen that when someone decides to be a devotee, he or she will immediately become as pure as driven snow, stripped overnight of all human faults and weaknesses as if by magic. When we really stop to think about it, the falsity of such a conclusion is ridiculously clear. Yes, we would all like to be transformed instantly and have all our faults removed. But even were this possible, such a drastic transformation would be far too severe a shock to the nervous system. Most human beings hate change and even more, hate uncertainty. This fact has been demonstrated very clearly in situations where a person will choose to stay in a difficult relationship, or an even dangerous situation, which has become familiar, rather than face an alternative that is Those unknown and therefore frightening because it involves insecurity.

Those who call themselves Sai devotees are just ordinary people who have come under the influence of Baba and his very practical teachings. They have not necessarily turned into angels overnight, much as we would all like to believe that would happen. So we must expect to see in the Sai Baba organization the same frictions, problems in communication, the same rivalry and competitiveness, and all the other problems encountered in any group of individuals.

Baba, himself, says that his organization is like a mini-version of the world, which can teach us how to relate to others who may have a very different idea about something that is in direct conflict with our own. As I have said before, one of Baba's sayings helps us to handle such differences of opinion. He says that we cannot always oblige another person if we do not agree with his or her motive or underlying belief, or lack of it. Also, we do not need to do what another person wants, for it may not be the correct action for us to follow. But, Baba continues, despite not always being able to acquiesce to someone's pressure, we must be careful how we express our refusal. We should always speak and act obligingly. This implies being firm and secure in our own position and what is right for each of us, but in a way that does not cause undue offense to the one coercing us, or cause him or her to feel insecure, threatened, or criticized harshly.

When we remember that Baba has assured us that at the core of our being we are all one, and therefore all of equal value, no one is qualified to condemn another.

However, we are all responsible for our own behavior and should try to live according to the teachings that have proved to be correct for each of us. It means that we remain firm and insist on the right to retain our own beliefs, and that we follow a correct course of action in harmony with it. This is our responsibility, so we must insist on the necessary freedom to pursue it. Those who choose to follow Baba must exercise the same caution with respect to other devotees. We should not allow anyone to persuade us to act at variance to his teachings.

How do we handle inappropriate behavior? We should not overlook wrong-doing when we recognize it, as to do so makes us as guilty as the wrong-doer. We could point out the wrong act in such a way that no offense is given, and no harsh judgment is implied. In that way we are absolved from any guilt resulting from silently appearing to approve of a wrong-ful act.

Living what we believe involves the heart and not merely the head. Of course we must use the brain to help us determine what is correct, but then the heart needs to be brought into play to balance the often cold, critical, or calculating attitude connected with the brain, for compassion, kindness, and willingness to help all spring from an open heart. If we are aware of what is right for everyone involved in any situation we stop centering only on what each member wants personally.

As mentioned previously, Baba says that people who are thrown together in a close relationship on a daily basis can help each other remove their rough edges. When stones or rocks are shaken together in a jar, they polish one another as they rub up against each other. Baba often relates this action to marriage, for the partners are being given the opportunity to be polished by the daily friction of their two separate wills and egos.

If this is true of a couple, it must be a great deal more accurate in a group that meets regularly. Here, the effect is greatly multiplied.

When I travel to the many different countries, I am often asked to visit Sai centers and give a talk about Baba. This gives me insight into the groups of people who are uniting in a joint effort to practice his teachings. These groups are composed of ordinary people who have been educated in a very different way from the education Baba proposes. They gather together and bring to each group their old patterns of thinking, speaking, and acting, which are, in most instances, in direct contradiction to Baba's. Baba advocates cooperation as opposed to operation. But most people have been indoctrinated with the idea that to be successful they must compete in order to be better and achieve more than anyone else. So, of course, the groups are, as Baba often points out, like mini-worlds or miniature examples of the larger world scene where competitiveness is rampant everywhere.

Baba tells us that his life is his message, and that our lives should also reflect this message. If we are able to correct the heart by-pass in our own lives, we will automatically reverse it in our activity in any group. In Sai groups, we have chosen to be his devotees, and it is very important to practice his teachings.

Are we treating others in the group with tolerance? Are we demonstrating a caring attitude in our interactions with others? Are we remembering that others may need our help? Are we cooperating amicably with the other members, or are we using our position as officers to allow our ego free rein to exert undue control over others?

Baba tells us that he is our servant, so if he willingly and lovingly assumes that role, we should follow his example and serve the members of the group by being willing to help without being critical or condescending. Each one is on an individual path back to our Source. We often do not consciously know where we are on this path, so we most certainly cannot know the progress (or lack of it) for anyone else. We need to exhibit patience, tolerance, steadfastness, and forbearance, and remember that family, friends, business associates, or members of the Sai organization can all be our teachers. If there were no problems we would have no challenges, and without challenges we cannot develop strength and resilience, or the Self-confidence that develops when we allow the Self to help us to find solutions.

CHAPTER 29

MAChiNES, CompuTERS ANd oTHER ElECTRONiC DEViCES THAT CONTRIbUTE TO THE HEART By-PASS

Our society is fast becoming dominated by machines of all descriptions, and these contribute considerably to the by-pass of the heart in all areas of life.

The most natural method of communication is speech. Originally such an exchange was limited to those who were physically present. For distant communication, letters were delivered by messengers, first on horseback or by boat, now by train or plane.

The invention of the telephone enabled us to speak to people living at a distance, and since then modern communication devices have proliferated. Some modern inventions have greatly enhanced our lives.

However, any good thing can be overdone, and now that electronic devices are in such wide use, it is common to hear machine-made messages from most businesses when we call. A recorded voice gives directions to press this or that number according to what the caller needs. Even after the choice has been made, there is usually a long wait before we can speak to an actual person. This lack of personal communication is further cutting us off from human contacts that used to be part of daily life. Instead, we are being forced to communicate with cold machines that lack human emotions, which may annoy or frustrate us, further adding to our own heart by-pass.

Computers are having a tremendous impact on all aspects of our lives, some beneficial, others intimidating. Computers have revolutionized business and simplified home accounting. Internet subscribers have access to information from around the world, with the possibility of interacting with other people on a global level. Medical information is now available world-wide through computers, making it possible for doctors to get the latest information on drugs and medical techniques at the touch of a finger.

As wonderful as computers may seem, anything that furthers the heart by-pass is harmful to us all. While computers open doors of learning for young people, the handicapped and elderly, they can become another means of escape when used as a substitute for caring relationships. Spending hours playing computer games or "surfing the Internet" can cause people to close their hearts to the world around them. Even the greatest literature and music contribute to the heart by-pass when used as an escape.

Computer users should monitor their time at the keyboard for this and various other reasons. Concentrated use of computers has recently been found to cause eye problems, especially in children whose eyes are still not fully developed. In addition, repetitive use of the fingers and wrists on computer keyboards set at the incorrect height can cause a painful, career-ending disability called carpel tunnel syndrome. It is also said that the aura around a computer affects our physical aura.

An even more serious problem is the availability of pornography on the Internet. Pornographic stories and pictures certainly add to the heart by-pass, and anyone who is indulging in this form of escapism is not only by-passing his or her own heart, but is also contributing to the dehumanizing thought form now prevalent in the world.

Since we will continue to live under the control of this mechanized structure, which will only increase with time, we will have to discover ways to work around it so that it does not prevent us from *re-connecting* our own hearts and making contact with other people with feeling, and not just with our brains, voices, and bodies.

Individually, we can decide to open our own hearts and, on a daily basis, direct the flow of love from the Source within us, whose very nature is love, to all those we meet as well as to those who live at a distance. If we practice this simple service daily, it will keep our own hearts open and will also help others to open their hearts.

Our personal love is inadequate compared to that of the Hi C. We have our limitations and our likes and dislikes, but Its love is completely accepting, nonjudgmental and deeply fulfilling. We can make a difference by letting the increasing take-over by machines remind us not to let our own cold, unfeeling brains take over our lives. By regularly setting aside a few minutes during the day to let love from the Hi C flow through us, we can do our part in correcting the universal imbalance between Yin and Yang by keeping our own hearts open.

CHAPTER 30

Traffic and Private and Public Transportation

Another area where the heart is most certainly absent is seen on the streets and freeways in any city. I live in Los Angeles, which is a city of automobiles, due to the fact that public transportation is minimal and most inadequate for the needs of so large an area. Many so-called freeways connect the various parts, but at the peak hours when commuters drive to and from their workplaces, the freeways are so crowded that they are far from being *free ways*. I am always highly amused when I am visiting other countries, and even other parts of the USA, when I hear complaints about the traffic. I laugh and say, "But at least we are moving, albeit slowly. I am used to sitting in a traffic jam intermittently starting and stopping with all four lanes of cars at a standstill."

Under such stressful conditions, drivers are frustrated, and the heart by-pass is very evident. Motorists cut in front of other cars in the vain hope of making time, though these drivers rarely make much headway. They often do not arrive at their destination any sooner, and there is the possibility that their impatience could cause an accident or result in a traffic ticket. Their actions may arouse anger or fear in other motorists, which closes off their hearts and leaves no room for love.

The heart by-pass is also seen when cars enter a freeway from an on-ramp without respecting the merge or yield signs. Safety rules direct cars to alternate, to allow those about to enter to do so safely. But many drivers fail to show consideration or even common sense when they are behind the wheel.

Cars and motorcycles frequently dart in and out between other cars. This practice can be extremely dangerous, especially when the vehicles are small and it is hard for other drivers to see their approach. Another traffic hazard is when cars swerve in front of trucks, overlooking the fact that a truck cannot stop as quickly as a car to avoid an accident.

Another hazard involves people who use portable telephones and carry on heated or animated conversations, waving their hands in the air and gesticulating to the invisible party at the other end of the telephone. Sometimes, they can also be seen leafing through papers from a briefcase placed on the seat beside them.

I have also noticed women busily applying make-up while driving, and both men and women combing their hair; some men even shave as they drive!

Some people play such loud music over the car radio or on a cassette that it prevents the driver from being able to hear even the piercing sound of a siren signalling the approach of an ambulance, fire truck, or police car.

An even more serious example of the lack of responsibility is when people insist on driving when they are under the influence of liquor, drugs, or any medication that is known to reduce their ability to think and act quickly in an emergency. While the traffic laws are quite strict with drunk drivers, they do not seem to take into account people on recreational drugs, or on medication. Some people taking medication are not even aware they should not be driving.

All of these examples show a lack of concern for the driver's safety and for the comfort and safety of others, particularly in rush-hour traffic, when complete concentration is essential. However, we cannot afford to be critical of the way other people drive if we are guilty of a similar lack of consideration and are only concentrating on reaching our destination at any cost. We need to become more aware of our own driving habits, and change them where necessary.

Travel by plane has become the most frequent means of transportation over long distances. Whereas travel by automobile places the driver in control, on a plane passengers are being carried to their destinations with no effort on their part. They therefore are not free to make choices that affect others.

Passengers are at the mercy of the airline company to provide the seating, food, air, and general comfort. It has become a well-known fact that the air in planes is recycled to save the cost of providing adequate but more expensive ventilation. Passengers are exposed to all kinds of airborne viruses and other hazards. Many people become ill after having flown in a commercial plane and are not always aware of the cause. The health and safety of these people has been overlooked by the airlines in preference to earning more money, again showing a lack of concern for the individual.

Then there is the rapidly increasing problem of air pollution that plagues densely-populated cities. Exhaust fumes that are constantly being spewed out from the thousands of private cars and commercial and public vehicles contaminate the air, rendering it unhealthy for the inhabitants.

Los Angeles, where I live, is one of the most polluted cities as far as smog is concerned. It is situated in a natural bowl with mountains and ocean surrounding it on all sides. This configuration creates an inversion, which causes contaminants from commercial sources, in addition to the fumes from the motorized vehicles, to be held closer to the ground during certain seasons of the year, creating a dense pall in which people live and breathe. Those who are sensitive suffer from allergic reactions with sinus congestion, headaches, nausea, dizziness, confused thinking, and a lack of energy.

When a plane in which I am returning from overseas starts to descend during one of these smoggy periods, I am always shocked to see the brownish layer which obscures from view the blue sky and clouds I used to love so much as a child and that can still be enjoyed in less polluted areas.

What a steep price to pay for progress! The absence of concern for the health of the world population has resulted in the present crisis with which we are now faced in so many areas. It involves unsafe air, water, and food, all of which we feel helpless to remedy on an individual basis. The quality of health, and therefore of our lives, is reduced drastically when the earth is becoming increasingly polluted due to our lack of concern for our environment.

It must be obvious to all concerned people that these are huge problems that can easily overwhelm us. We may wonder how we can begin to make a difference and help to *re-connect* the heart.

We can start by making changes in our own behavior. For instance, we can make a difference in our driving habits by being more considerate of other drivers and by acknowledging with a wave or a smile when they are courteous to us. We can stay off the highways when we have been drinking or when we are on medication. We can do our small part in cutting pollution by combining trips when we have errands to run. We can carpool or use public transportation when possible.

These are just a few changes we can make in our daily lives to help start the process. It all begins by opening our own hearts and being more kind and considerate, which in turn helps to open the hearts of others.

Chapter 31

The Media

What is our main influence today? I think most people would agree that it is TV. This modern invention is used to educate and entertain. TV exposes many people to information they might otherwise never have a chance to acquire. It requires none of the costly fees charged for lectures or classes. It is available in the home so that members of a family do not even need to leave their residence, also eliminating the cost of transportation and parking. People can watch TV in very casual dress in the privacy of their home. TV is therefore a most seductive way to absorb information. This is all very positive, but unfortunately, there are many programs available for public viewing that leave much to be desired in regard to the overall influence on those who choose to watch them.

Directors and producers of television and motion pictures have the opportunity to reach literally millions of individuals in every country. Positive and uplifting messages could help change the grim situation so prevalent in today's world. But instead, TV programs and movies that encourage the most base instincts and emotions reach a vast audience. This is particularly dangerous in its effect on children and young people, for the young absorb everything they see or hear without the benefit of discrimination, which is developed later in life. Young people are exposed daily in their own homes to negative messages that do not offer them a balanced view of life.

One of the excuses usually given for providing violent and negative entertainment is that people demand it. Networks and movie distributors obviously want to attract the largest number of possible customers, so they try to reach the widest audience.

In the reverie work, I have been taught that we receive impressions on the subconscious level of our minds, though we may not always be aware of doing so. This is true even when we are asleep or unconscious. Many parents allow babies and very small children to watch TV for hours at a time to keep them occupied and quiet and out of the parents' way. The children are being exposed to negative conditioning, whether or not they understand it with their conscious minds. It all goes directly to the subconscious level where it remains undigested or unprocessed by the conscious mind. This can cause all kinds of psychological and emotional problems later in life. This habit is a clear example of the way some parents close their hearts to the welfare of their children when they allow them to watch inappropriate programs.

Programs of a negative or exploitative nature are being beamed at the general public with no care or consideration for their effect on the millions of people who watch them. So, instead of being the positive influence it once promised to be, TV has now become a mixed blessing, as it is capable of influencing people around the world in a negative way.

But the networks are not entirely to blame for this state of affairs. As they say, they give to the public whatever they are asked to provide, so we are the ones who can change the tone of the programs by requesting fare that is more conducive to improving the minds of the audience instead of debasing them.

TV soap operas, romantic novels, movies, and plays are frequently used as a form of escape from everyday life. Many people identify with the characters portrayed on the screen, or in print, and vicariously live the more exciting lives portrayed, but it poses no challenge to the viewers. It allows them to avoid relationships with actual people. Again, it is one-sided, as they have complete control of the imaginary interaction, so the heart is closed to the many real people in their lives with whom it could be possible for them to interact.

Advertising has increasingly become part of today's media, and it, too, has an enormous effect on people of all ages. Young children are easily seduced by it and clamor for their parents to buy the products that are dangled before their eyes on the TV screen, or in newspapers, magazines, and catalogs.

Very little consideration appears to be given to the probable effect a product may have on the purchasers, or even whether the advertisement carries an honest statement of its worth or usefulness. It would seem that the main concern is to lure as many customers as possible to buy the wares in order to guarantee the maximum amount of profit for the advertisers.

Advertising, as such, is not the problem. We all need to know that certain commodities are available and where they can be obtained. On the other hand, the dishonest description of a product and what it will accomplish for the buyer is misleading, especially when aimed at children. They, of course, present a most tempting target to increase the sales of the products being displayed on screens in thousands of living rooms all over the world. The lure of a larger audience is sufficiently tempting to out-weigh any possible misgivings about the effect of the products on the children who are being persuaded to possess them. It is a well-known fact that children are extremely impressionable and want whatever they see advertised, particularly when their peers have these articles.

This sets the stage for a future belief that owning these "desirable" things can bring happiness. Advertisers who have closed hearts are both feeding into this mistaken belief and using it for profit.

Another media influence that is particularly strong in the lives of children and young people is music. As stated in the chapter on the treatment of animals, it has been demonstrated that even plants react to music, so this must surely be true for human beings, especially young people who are still impressionable. It was observed that classical music caused plants to turn or lean toward the music. But with certain kinds of percussive, or very loud music, such as rock & roll, and rap, the plants tried to move as far away from the sound as possible.

Yet children and young people wear earphones and listen to this music for hours at a time. Loud music reportedly can have an adverse effect on hearing. In addition to the effect on the ears from the music and its hypnotic beat, today's lyrics often contain material that is extremely negative in its impact, especially for young children. Though they may not always consciously understand the messages the lyrics contain, children are being programmed on the subconscious level with thoughts of violence, profanity, and a complete absence of caring for others. It has been observed that some young children are prone to violent words and actions even when they are not aware of their meaning.

In Baba's Ceiling on Desires Program, he points out that food includes not only what we eat or drink, but everything that we ingest through each of the five sense organs: eyes, ears, nose, mouth, and skin. Whatever we see, hear, taste, breathe in, or touch acts as another kind of food.

More and more we are being alerted to the importance of care in the selection of what we eat and drink and the elimination of those items that are known to have a deleterious effect on our physical health. In addition, we would be wise to become educated about the possible effect the many other kinds of "food" that Baba refers to may have on us.

The two main categories include all that we see and everything we hear. What do we allow to enter through our eyes when we watch TV, movies and plays, or when we read books, magazines, and newspapers that might cause unpleasant reactions now, or at some time in the future?

What do we take in through our ears that could have an adverse effect on our health and comfort? Listening to questionable radio programs and certain kinds of music, participating in conversations involving gossip, criticism of others, or salacious stories, all come under this heading.

We are free to choose what we ingest in any or all of these ways. It is our responsibility to exercise discrimination and caution when making decisions for ourselves and for the members of our family. That means considering the welfare of each one and not only what is easy or convenient for ourselves. This is one way to keep an open heart instead of relying solely on our thinking ability when making decisions that affect other people.

Chapter 32

Charisma and the Myth of the Public Image

There is a kind of myth that has been created around certain people, of which the person involved is often unaware. It is composed of other people's observations, both true and erroneous about an individual, his or her life, contacts, possessions, relationships, and everything else that others have projected onto the individual, or, in some cases, that he or she has deliberately created. This false image is a thought form woven from many people's opinions and desires which, therefore, rarely accurately represents the person.

The most obvious examples of this phenomenon are people who are highly visible, and include movie stars and public performers of all kinds—politicians, musicians, authors, sports personalities, lecturers, artists, and many others who in some way are in the public eye. These people are discussed at length and in depth in the various media. The most minute details of news concerning them is collected and evaluated by the general public.

Television has added vastly to this phenomenon by presenting to millions of viewers around the world anyone and everyone who appears to be of importance, either positively or negatively. Now, with the advent of computer networks, the visibility will be greatly increased as celebrity news is becoming available on the Internet.

The underlying theme is that these so-called famous people are more special or more important in the eyes of the world than anyone else, just because the spotlight has been projected onto them. People who worship the public figure hope that some of the glamor will rub off and provide them with the recognition they crave.

Publicly acclaimed figures are the butt of an onslaught of contradictory evaluations. They are copied by those who aspire to similar fame and denounced by those who are jealous or threatened by their success. This dual and conflicting mass projection creates an intense stress for many of these heros and heroines, who sometimes crack beneath the weight of others' scrutiny of their every word or act.

An example that comes immediately to mind is Princess Diana of England. She is constantly watched by millions, and alternately admired or criticized, both to an exaggerated extent. She represents a dream for multitudes of women who long to be in her position; for equally numerous men she represents the ideal partner. To some she can do no wrong, while to others she is the object of constant and widespread gossip and criticism. But neither of these projected images presents a true picture of who she really is.

Many people indulge in fantasy relationships with charismatic figures, to take the place of actual ones. In some ways it is easier to fantasize having a perfect relationship with a romantic figure, as it poses none of the problems encountered with the actual people in their lives, as no real interaction is involved.

Some people's infatuation with a public figure develops into an obsession that has been known to lead to violence when the chosen idol does not reciprocate. This situation is extreme, but many people indulge in one-sided fantasy relationships to a lesser degree. When personal relationships do not live up to their hopes, people become infatuated with either a public figure or someone in their lives who seems to meet their expectations.

Such one-sided relationships remind me of the difference between a game of tennis played with a partner and the solitary pastime of batting a ball against a wall with no one else involved.

We need to look at our own reactions to charismatic figures to see if we are idealizing them because we are not happy with our relationships. On the other hand, we need to see if we are being overly critical of public figures in order to feel better about ourselves. Either way, it is a form of escape that keeps us from connecting with everyone and everything in our lives with open hearts.

CHAPTER 33

THE FALLACY OF SELF-IMPORTANCE AND THE IMPORTANCE OF SELF-IMPORTANCE

As I have pointed out earlier, competitiveness is everywhere evident. It permeates every area of life and causes undue stress to both individuals and groups who are under pressure to excel in some way. Such stress is particularly harmful for children and teenagers in the process of developing and discovering themselves to determine how they will fit into society.

To be better than someone else and, in extreme cases, to be better than everyone else in some feat, either physical or mental, has become the goal to be achieved; the be-all and end-all of life.

The purpose of life is not winning and competition or being self-important; in fact it is the exact opposite. Each person's life presents an opportunity to learn specific lessons, detach from false beliefs, and grow toward union with the Real Self, which is the motivating factor within everyone, whether we are conscious of this fact or not. At the level of the Real Self, we all are of equal value, neither more nor less important than anyone else. But the idea of Self-Importance is extremely difficult for many people to accept, because the ego's *raison d'etre* is to be important and in control. The ego fears to be deposed in favor of the Hi C, and will fight to retain its position of authority. This battle for supremacy rages within most people, and causes anger, depression, envy, jealousy, intolerance, cruelty, and a host of other militant emotions to emerge, sometimes as a complete surprise. When people visit Sai Baba at his ashram, this process is often greatly exacerbated to the intense astonishment and embarrassment of everyone concerned.

One time, while we were at the ashram, I recall an American woman who was behaving in a most inappropriate manner. She was speaking in a very loud voice, calling out to Baba, and generally flouting the few ashram rules intended to preserve order among the vast crowds that gather for Baba's darshan. Many people, but particularly some of the younger ones, were upset that she was allowed to behave in such a discourteous way, especially when they were admonished to obey the rules. They were also upset that Baba even seemed to approve, and gave her a lot of attention. One of the members of the U.S. Sai organization elected to ask Baba about this puzzling problem. Baba smiled sweetly and said that he purposely gave the woman attention to stir up jealousy and envy in other devotees who did not even know they had such negative emotions as they were so well hidden. So he used her to help other devotees become aware of their own hidden negativity. He does not hesitate to use anyone to instill his teachings, for we all learn from one another.

It appears that Baba's tremendous energy and expansive and all-embracing love stir up subconscious emotions, attitudes, and behavior patterns in people who want to feel self-important. But Baba teaches Self Importance, which means that we are all equal at the High Self level. As Baba says,"There may be differences among men in physical strength, financial status, intellectual acumen—but all are equal in the eye of God."

Many people want to feel special or self-important and be treated as a VIP. What is a VIP, and who are these "very important people" who seem to be everywhere? Some are well known public figures and some are not; some are merely referred to obliquely, as in a VIP section railed off at some special function.

Unfortunately, the yardstick by which VIPs are measured is usually a worldly one, which rates wealth, social or political importance, physical beauty, mental acuity, power, prowess in a sport, acting or singing ability, above service and true philanthropy, unselfishness, and other positive qualities that include caring and love. The VIP label is attached to the "small self" and places value on qualities that are admired by the general public. But since the visible personality is only the shell that contains the real person, adulation afforded to a VIP is a waste of time. It leads those who indulge in such hero-worship to evaluate other people from a superficial level.

Treating others as VIPs contributes to the heart by-pass. The hearts of those made to feel less important are often closed because they feel inferior, while the hearts of the so-called VIPs are also closed when they are made to feel superior.

There are actually no VIPs, for we are all equal at the center of our being. When this truth is experienced, the heart can be *re-connected*, and used to express the universal love it is so perfectly designed to do. In this way, the heart by-pass will eventually be healed at the individual, and, then, automatically at the world level.

CHAPTER 34

BE HAPPY

Baba tells us to be happy
No matter what life brings,
If it's something to our liking
Such as people, jobs or things,

Or if its something painful
That makes us want to cry
And in certain situations
To wish that we could die.

But Baba says we're free to choose
The attitude to take
And that it's always up to us
Which choices we will make.

He says the road on which we walk
Is a bumpy one at best,
Going up when we are happy
And down when we're depressed.

We get puffed up when things go well
And punctured when we're sad.
So why not walk a smoother path
And accept both good and bad?

Baba will often say to someone, "Be happy." As I look back
over the many visits to India, I realize that this injunction runs
like a thread through his discourses, interviews, and the ca-

sual meetings during darshan. It is one of the most important of his many teachings.

We tend to take ourselves far too seriously. Many of us spend our lives bowed down under heavy burdens that are like weighty backpacks. We rationalize this tendency and call it "taking responsibility." But Baba refers to it as "excess luggage."

We may believe that if we find the right partner to love us we will live happily ever after, as the fairy tales promised. We seek money and all the great variety of things money enables us to buy. We overeat. Food is often substituted in a vain attempt to secure happiness, if only temporarily. Indulgence in alcohol and drugs may provide a fleeting sense of that most sought-after carefree feeling that we equate with happiness. We often hear the phrase, "I will be happy if...." But the sources of the hoped-for happiness are generally external, whereas Baba teaches that true and lasting happiness is possible only when sought from within.

What prevents us from achieving that state of being which we all crave and eagerly seek, but rarely succeed in finding? When we are faced with a situation that we do not like, or do not know how to handle, we feel threatened and inadequate. We lose our sense of well-being, and are no longer happy. When we fail to get what we want, whether it is an object, a personal relationship, or something less tangible—such as a promotion, an honor, a recognition, an opportunity to succeed in some way, or just to get our own way—again, we lose our sense of satisfaction and become unhappy.

Happiness cannot be given to us permanently by anything or anyone outside of ourselves, as it has to well up from within from our Source. This source of happiness is called Love.

If we really want to be happy, one of the surest ways to achieve it is to open up our hearts and let the love which is our true being flow out to reach all who are ready to receive it. It is actually a very simple practice and one that involves remarkably little expenditure of time and energy, yet the rewards are unexpectedly gratifying, as I have learned from experience.

For instance, instead of seeking, expecting, or even demanding love from specific chosen people, as so many of us do, I direct the love from the Hi C to everyone I know and those I meet. When I remember to do so, I find that love literally pours back to me from the most unexpected sources. People are all hungry for love, but have so often been disappointed with the human variety when the motive is a selfish one. When they feel the love from the Hi C, which is unconditional and has no strings attached, they can safely open up their hearts to receive it. Then they are able to direct it to other people. In fact, when we are willing to practice it, the results are often most surprising. We may find that people with whom we have had difficulties seem to change and that the relationship improves considerably.

Work as Worship

I have covered only a few of the main areas where the heart by-pass is so dramatically evident throughout the world. But there are, of course, many more that I have been obliged to omit for the sake of brevity. We can find examples in our own lives which will be different for each of us.

As more and more people enter the workplace, each of us would do well to check our behavior to catch sight of instances where we are, maybe unconsciously, primarily using our brains and intellect and over-looking the need to include our hearts and feelings. It is imperative to balance the reasoning ability with consideration for the effect that any enterprise or action we initiate may have on everyone involved.

Since it is obvious that in our many past appearances in the world in human form we have all contributed to the present state of the world, we are all now responsible for helping to *re-connect* the heart or Yin energy in our personal lives. Then we can bring more kindness, consideration, and understanding to the people in the various work groups and social circles of which we are a part. This, in turn, will help to *re-connect* the heart in our own country and eventually in the world.

This positive and active approach will reap greater rewards than if we continue to lament the problems we see in our present situation and blame other people, whether the government and politicians, or our own supervisors and coworkers. We can directly change only our own behavior and bring it into balance. This will indirectly result in changes in the workplace and further afield.

When problems arise at work, it is often because people have trouble communicating or relating to a co-worker. A company puts pressure on a supervisor, who, in turn, puts pressure on the workers. Many companies actually function in an atmosphere of competition and fear. When the heart is bypassed in a company, each of the individual workers is adversely affected. To counteract such a negative situation, I often advocate that people do as I did in the hi-jacking experience: direct love from the Hi C to any workers with whom they are experiencing problems.

We also need to bear in mind two important factors that affect our work: First, we are all being faced with our past actions and can learn now what we failed to learn in a past experience, and secondly, we can be used to bring a glimmer of light to the workplace when we allow the love of the Hi C to open our own hearts. This can be like a chain reaction and open the hearts of those with whom we work, expanding into their lives and, in turn, affecting people we may never know.

Baba advocates treating work as worship. If we follow this advice we can stop seeing work as drudgery and allow ourselves to be used as an instrument of our real Self, Baba Self or Hi C.

Many people complain that they find their daily life dull and boring and the future appears to be depressing and without hope of improvement. This seems to be the chief complaint of those who eagerly awaited the time when they would finally reach the age of retirement. For many years they had anticipated being free from the daily grind. They looked forward to a life of leisure. But to their great disappointment they find that they miss the former daily routine supplied by their occupation. They discover that continuous leisure can be both boring and unfulfilling. So they are often reduced to becoming malcontents and are even more frustrated than when they were gainfully employed in a regular routine. Many men sicken and die at a comparatively early age.

When we do as Baba suggests and approach work as worship, we can be directed from within while we are still working. This will prepare us to continue to be used as an instrument of the Real Self when we retire.

I often jokingly comment that Baba pays no attention to old age or retirement. Many of his devotees are involved in various activities until they die.

I have found from my own experience that when the Hi C is accepted as the guide, life becomes a continuous adventure with many surprises along the way. There is no time to be bored or to feel useless.

CHAPTER 36

CRACKED URN, BROKEN REED OR THE STONE THE BUILDER REJECTED?

This chapter is included to reassure all those readers who feel inadequate in some way. Many years ago when I was working with a partner using the reverie technique which we had been taught, I was suddenly confronted with the image of a cracked urn or vase. It had obviously been broken into hundreds of pieces which had been painstakingly fitted together and glued back into the shape of the original vessel.

I wondered why this particular image was being revealed to me, so I asked to be given the reason. The answer I received gave me such an emotional shock that I burst into tears. I was shown that I was like that cracked and patched urn. I was both horrified and deeply depressed at such a thought. I had always been perfectly aware that my physical body had, ever since childhood, caused me many problems and a great deal of pain, but to have it so starkly illustrated was quite unnerving. Then, at the height, or—to be more accurate—at the depth of the shock, came another message from within. The urn represented the physical sheath in which resided the light or Real Self, and that inner light could shine through all the cracks with no hindrance. Other insights continued, and I realized that in those areas where we fail, are weak or inept, the light can operate, whereas in successful or strong areas, the ego (and pride) get in the way, blocking the light from shining through. In those areas where we know we cannot succeed, we are generally sufficiently humble to ask for help. When we are successful, it does not occur to us to defer to the wisdom within. It is not what the physical vehicle expresses that is important, but what the Hi C is able to express through all the avenues or cracks that are available. So everyone has an opportunity to allow It to use their faults and weaknesses. When the Hi C is given the chance to express Itself through even the weakest and smallest vessel, the world will feel the effect. Like the Hundredth Monkey, when only one person allows this to happen, the world can change for the better.

So what are the avenues or windows through which the Hi C is expressed? Each life gives us the opportunity to learn a certain lesson or lessons. It also allows us to hand over the direction of all our many aspects to the guidance of the Hi C. When this is done, even the least probable vessel can be used to emit the light through its very cracks or imperfections. So, why do we hesitate to let this happen?

This entire experience had a very strong impact on me as soon as the original shock at being shown that I, myself, was like a cracked urn had somewhat subsided. I am painfully aware that I have many weaknesses, and the knowledge had always depressed me because I had no idea how to strengthen them. Now I was being shown that they could be used by the Hi C to reveal Itself. Yes, I was a most unlikely vessel to be used, as anyone who knew me then would have agreed. But the Hi C can use anyone who is willing to be Its instrument, and It can create miracles through the most cracked vessels.

The body/ego/personality is like the essential scaffolding around a building under construction. As soon as the building is completed, the scaffolding is no longer needed. When we allow the light or love to shine forth, we will no longer need the physical scaffolding, lamp shade, or body, as the light is the only reality. Suddenly I understood the significance of a quotation from the bible I had often heard repeated as a child. "The stone which the builders rejected has become the chief cornerstone" (Psalms 118.22). And "Nor do men light a lamp and put it under a bushel" (Matthew 5.15).

As I look back over the past year, while I have been trying to let this book be written through me as the instrument in the hands of Baba or the Hi C, I wonder how it has ever been accomplished. Never in all my long life have I traveled overseas so many times in so short a period to give seminars on my work and talks about Baba. It has left me very little time to concentrate on writing. In addition, I have never suffered from such continuous health and dental problems as has been the case this year. On top of these delays, I have had to take over everything my husband used to do before he died.

I am certain that I have not always been adequate to the tasks even as an instrument. But it is we who often demand perfection, both from others and ourselves. Either of such expectations is but another way the ego tries to take over control. Baba tells us that if we dedicate everything to God and become instruments, we will incur no further karma from these activities, since we will no longer be the doer.

However, that does not necessarily mean that we have worked out all the past karma that we have put into action in our many past lives. I am always astonished when someone announces with a smugly satisfied smile that this is their last life and that he or she is going to merge with Baba. How presumptuous! We are not in a position to know whether this will be the case, or even where we are in regard to balancing our karma. So instead of resting on our imaginary laurels in such a hope or belief, which is the ultimate ego trip, we need to work on this present life. Only this life gives us the opportunity to allow our Real Self to use us as instruments, and whenever the time has come, to absorb our personalities into It.

Again, it is a matter of "Thy will; not mine."

Readers of *Sai Baba: The Ultimate Experience* have repeatedly asked me whether I still suffer from the incapacitating headaches I had for most of my life. Baba had told me they were from five different causes, and that he would help me. Yes, I am happy to be able to report that they did eventually disappear, one by one, over a period of about ten years from the date of his first diagnosis. However, they represented only one of the physical infirmities which I had brought with me into this life for my learning.

I have often asked Baba about my less-than-comfortable health, and he has given me various responses over the years whenever we visited him. At our first visit he told me that the body must be made strong before enlightenment could be possible. On another visit he informed me that the problems were not mental but were physical-mechanical in origin. That was a partial relief, but certainly did little to alleviate the distress. At a later interview he explained that my body could be likened to the Kurukshetra, the battlefield described in the Indian classic, the *Bhagavad-Gita*, where the battle between the two opposing armies of good and evil took place. That, too, was only slight consolation.

On another occasion he looked around at the group awaiting an interview where my husband and I were the only Westerners, all the others being Indian. When his eyes alighted on me he made a grimace and announced to the assembled group, "Poor Mrs. Krystal has a bad stomach," while relishing the fact that at the time I still had a horror of a spotlight being shone on me. Not content with that comment, he added, "Not only a bad stomach but a bad head, bad eyes, bad back and bad feet." To my intense surprise I answered, "If it is all *karmic*, please help me to finish it all as soon as possible," at which the whole group, including Baba, laughed out loud at such a request.

Baba has made many other similar remarks and on several instances has materialized healing ash, called *vibhuti*, and pills of various shapes and sizes, but all so far apparently to no avail. Then just as I was putting the finishing touches to this book an answer was forthcoming that was startlingly simple and obviously true.

I had been particularly indisposed for several weeks and lacked the energy to do anything apart from the bare essentials, when a close friend called to tell me that he, too, had been feeling very depressed. He was helpless to curb his various appetites, and was wondering if we could work on it to find some help. I told him I doubted that I was well enough to trust anything that came to me as issuing from the Hi C and not from my confused mind, but that I was willing to try to ask for help for both of us.

The first thing that came to my mind after we had settled quietly and asked to be helped was a strange split image of each of us. It was as if we were standing to one side of another part of us that was like a twin, except that this second part was less solid or dense and more luminous. The instruction that came was that we were to contemplate this double image, which we did, though it was not clear to either of us what it was actually intended to reveal.

After sitting quietly for several minutes the explanation started to flow into my mind.

First, I was shown that although my friend and I were not at all alike and had seemingly very different problems, we had one condition in common. We were both being controlled by our bodies, mine by various physical-mechanical conditions, and his by appetites. We had never realized this similarity before, and would undoubtedly never have thought of it, so it was a complete surprise to both of us, even though we readily understood its significance and correctness as soon as it was brought to our combined attention.

Further explanation continued to flow into my mind that we had both exerted extreme control over others in former lives, though each at a different time and place. We were now being controlled by our own physical bodies from which, however much we might try, we could not escape except in death.

What could be more exquisitely fitting than to be under the control of the very vehicle that had been fashioned from former actions and in which we were now living? So what could we do about it? Surrender, trust, and accept until we have finished whatever it will take to reverse it.

So let us allow the Hi C to take over at the helm of our ship, which symbolizes the Yin or feeling way through life, as well as the steering wheel of our car, or the Yang or thinking way through life. Then we can allow It to *re-connect* our hearts and send Its love through them to flow out into the world.

Epilogue

Just as I was finishing the manuscript of this book, a most interesting and significant delay occurred, which epitomizes the subject matter in a very grim way.

Baba had sent me a message through a friend who was returning from India, which he had repeated to him on two separate occasions. The message was for me to attend the Guru-Purnima festival in July. I immediately recognized that Baba was following the same pattern with this book as he had with the previous ones. With each one he has told me to take the manuscript to him for his blessing, and as soon as it was published to return to present him with a copy of the book.

So now he had supplied me with a deadline: the manuscript had to be ready to take with me when I would leave for India early in July.

As soon as I had finished the manuscript, it was sent by express mail to Peggy Lenney, who has so carefully typed several of my other books into her computer. When it did not arrive the day after it had been mailed, she called to tell me. The succeeding day, when it had still not arrived, she decided to call her local post office to inquire the reason for its delay. She was informed that it was being detained at the central distribution center, together with all the other packages that had been delivered there. It was explained that a warning had been received by authorities that another bomb was about to be sent through the mail. Some of the previous bombs had injured and even killed the recipients of these lethal parcels. No chances could be taken, so all pieces of mail of a size that might contain a bomb were detained until they could be in-spected.

That this bomb scare should have happened just as I had finished and mailed the manuscript of this book could not have been accidental.

What could be a clearer example of the heart by-pass than knowingly to send out bombs that maim or kill the unfortu-nate recipients into whose hands one of these packages would land? This is an extreme case of hate being sent out instead of love. This one act had a widespread impact on an untold num-ber of people.

Fortunately, few of us are so intensely negative, but ac-tions such as this one can alert each of us to our own behav-ior, so that we can check it for any negativity of which we may not yet have been aware. We are all capable of sending out thoughts, feelings, words and actions that are harmful to other people, even if we would hesitate to send them an actual bomb.

When we look at all the instances of the heart by-pass that are so evident in the world, some of which have been alluded to in this book, we often feel helpless to make a differ-ence. But we need to bear in mind that the sum total of the influence of many separate individuals all opening their hearts and sending out love and kindness in the place of fear and hate *will* make a difference.

I am reminded of the mouse and the mountain of cheese. When faced with the stupendous task of eating an entire moun-tain of its favorite food, it was overwhelmed and already de-feated before it could even begin. But when advised to con-centrate on one small bite at a time, the whole mountain was finally demolished.

It is similar with the world scene. Each of us can accom-plish our small individual part by allowing the love to flow from our hearts to every person we meet. When enough people practice this daily routine, the world *must* change.

In this way, we can unite our efforts and contribute to a positive universal thought form composed of love, kindness, empathy, and caring. This will counteract the immense collec-tive negative thought form composed of hate, violence, spite, and meanness that hovers over the world. Since we have contributed to this negativity during our many lives over the centuries, we are affected by it now.

In one of Baba's oft-repeated sayings, he stresses the need for "Co-operation: not operation." Operation usually involves one person who plans and controls a project and oversees its progress until it is completed. Co-operation involves many people uniting in a joint effort toward a certain goal.

So let us all cooperate to make the difference and re-connect the love energy by opening up our hearts.

Phyllis Krystal is a psychotherapist. She was born in England but lives and works in California where she has developed her own techniques of psychotherapy. For over thirty years, she has been developing a counseling method using symbols and visualization techniques that help people detach from external authority figures and patterns in order to rely on their own Higher Consciousness as guide and teacher. To teach the method, Krystal gives lectures and seminars in the U. S., Europe, England, New Zealand, Tasmania, South America, and Australia. She is a devotee of Sathya Sai Baba, a world-renowned avatar living in India whose teachings and personal influence have been an inspiration. She is the author of *Cutting the Ties that Bind, Cutting More Ties that Bind, Sai Baba: The Ultimate Experience, Taming Our Monkey Mind,* and *Cutting the Ties that Bind Workbook,* also by Weiser.